BFI Film Classics

The BFI Film Classics series introduces, interprets and celebrates landmarks of world cinema. Each volume offers an argument for the film's 'classic' status, together with discussion of its production and reception history, its place within a genre or national cinema, an account of its technical and aesthetic importance, and in many cases, the author's personal response to the film.

For a full list of titles in the series, please visit
https://www.bloomsbury.com/uk/series/bfi-film-classics

T0346963

This book is dedicated to all trans, non-binary, gay, lesbian, bisexual, Black, of colour, disabled, sex worker, indigenous, survivor, working-class and women Star Wars fans – in all their constellations of identity and presentation. It is written, with love, for all the galaxy's orphans; to all those who fight for equality and justice despite being marginalized or underrepresented or told they don't belong. May our alliances be strong. May our resistance be hopeful. May the Force be with us. Always.

The Empire Strikes Back

Rebecca Harrison

THE BRITISH FILM INSTITUTE
Bloomsbury Publishing Plc
50 Bedford Square, London, WC1B 3DP, UK
1385 Broadway, New York, NY 10018, USA
29 Earlsfort Terrace, Dublin 2, Ireland

BLOOMSBURY is a trademark of Bloomsbury Publishing Plc

First published in Great Britain 2020 by Bloomsbury
Reprinted in 2020, 2025
on behalf of the
British Film Institute
21 Stephen Street, London, W1T 1LN
www.bfi.org.uk

The BFI is the lead organisation for film in the UK and the distributor of Lottery funds for film.
Our mission is to ensure that film is central to our cultural life, in particular by supporting and
nurturing the next generation of film-makers and audiences. We serve a public role which covers
the cultural, creative and economic aspects of film in the UK.

Cover artwork © Audrey Estok
Series cover design: Louise Dugdale
Series text design: ketchup/SE14
Images from *The Empire Strikes Back* (Irvin Kershner, 1980), © 1980 Lucasfilm Ltd/Twentieth
Century Fox Film Corporation.

A catalogue record for this book is available from the British Library.

A catalog record for this book is available from the Library of Congress.

ISBN: PB: 978-1-9112-3997-0
         ePDF: 978-1-9112-3996-3
         ePUB: 978-1-9112-3999-4

Typeset by Integra Software Services Pvt. Ltd.
Printed and bound in Great Britain

To find out more about our authors and books visit
www.bloomsbury.com and sign up for our newsletters.

Contents

Acknowledgments

It would not be possible to do this work without the emotional support of my friends and family. Thanks to Debbie Armour, Alex Neilson, Sophie Sexon, (Big) Emma Cardwell, (Wee) Emma Spence, Joanna Helfer, Arild Giske, Kyle Lonsdale, and (Sarah) Pickles, the best coven a chaotic writer with an impending deadline could hope for (even when you don't all know who Rian Johnson is). Thanks, as ever, to Lizzie Lay and Todd Wisdom for indulging all the midnight Star Wars screenings, even when you had to get up for work the next day. May the tiny Death Star chocolates be with you. Thanks to my parents – first and foremost for their love, but second and no less importantly for all the hours they endured watching *Ewoks* cartoons when I was a child. Thanks also to my sisters, for a more innocent time in our childhood when we thought the prequels were the height of brilliance (it's working … IT'S WOR-KING!).

Thanks, too, to all the academics, friends, and online acquaintances who have contributed in large and small ways to this project. Thanks to Hannah Hamad and David Martin-Jones for their comments and feedback on drafts. Thanks to Shira Peltzman for her archive suggestions, and to her and Ben for the use of their sofa while doing research in LA. Thanks to Lisa Kelly, Azadeh Emadi, Lizelle Bisschoff, Amy Holdsworth, Anna Backman-Rogers, Julia McClure, and the many other feminist friends and colleagues who have challenged and inspired my thinking. Thanks are also due to the film history community for its generous impulse to share knowledge and resources (thanks to Keith Johnston and Sheldon Hall, among others, for the loan of VHS and other materials). And, for her unceasing kindness, and for reading drafts and listening to my ideas and always asking the right (if unexpected) questions, thanks to Melanie Selfe.

Yours and Conor's support, wine supplies, and midnight lasagnes have provided much-needed intellectual sustenance throughout this project.

I also extend my warmest thanks to all the unsung guardians of the sacred texts: the librarians and curators who made this work possible (particularly Wendy Russell at the BFI, the team at the Margaret Herrick Library, and Lucas Seastrom at Lucasfilm); to interviewee Terri Hardin who is keeping the Star Wars fandom alive; to Audrey Estok for her beautiful cover art; and to Rebecca Barden and her team at Bloomsbury, without whom this project wouldn't have seen the light.

And finally, I would like to thank the enormous, diverse, and supportive Star Wars community – the Star Wars Representation Matters writers, the Looking for Leia crew, Amy Richau's 365 Days of Star Wars project, and the plethora of feminist and queer podcasts. Star Wars is for girls, people of colour, queer people, disabled people ... in short, all of us.

Notes on the Text

Given the amorphous nature of the Star Wars movies as a result of their various rereleases, I think it is helpful to clarify which versions of the films I refer to throughout this book.

Unless otherwise stated, all references to the original trilogy films (1977–83), including *The Empire Strikes Back*, are based on the original theatrical versions that are available on bonus discs as part of the 2008 Star Wars Special Edition box set. I have referred to the original theatrical versions to ensure that my analysis is as historically accurate as possible.

Owing to my historical approach (and in keeping with press, publicity, and general convention in 1980 when *Empire* was released), I refer to *Episode IV: A New Hope* as, simply, *Star Wars*. Whereas *Star Wars* in italics refers to the film, Star Wars, without italics, refers to the franchise. For example: viewers saw *Star Wars* in 1977; the Star Wars franchise includes films, games, and TV shows. Furthermore, to aid the consistency of the reading experience, I have amended all titles in primary documents to share a uniform format, for example 'Box Office for "Empire Strikes Back" Outperforms "Star Wars"', becomes 'Box Office for *Empire Strikes Back* Outperforms *Star Wars*'.

For further information about Star Wars screen media, as well as summaries of major characters and components of *The Empire Strikes Back*, please see the Glossary of Terms.

Introduction

Avid fans wait in impatient lines that zigzag around blocks outside movie theatres. Television broadcasters hover around queues of people that disrupt the flow of movement along city streets. Advertisements, on-set photographs, and talent interviews are emblazoned across the pages of magazines in a blitzkrieg media campaign; Darth Vader glares out from the cover of *Time*. A production legendary for its near-impossible location shoot and challenging visual effects has wrapped, and the industry waits, watching, as the film-makers launch that tricky thing – a sequel – on a trajectory to hoped-for box-office success. Deviating from its wildly popular predecessor in style and tone, no one knows what to expect. It is 21 May 1980, and suddenly there is a disturbance in the Force. The cinema doors open at long last. The first lucky viewers are admitted and scramble into their seats...

The Empire is about to strike back.

What began life as a risky sequel to the 1977 blockbuster hit *Star Wars* is now just one film in a canonical saga that encompasses three trilogies, two spin-offs, five television shows, numerous arcade and console games, theme park rides, comics, novels, documentaries, and innumerable toys and merchandise. Yet forty years after its first theatrical release, *The Empire Strikes Back* (henceforth, *Empire*) is now widely regarded as the best Star Wars film. The movie regularly tops polls and critically curated lists in newspapers and on fan websites.[1] It appears in popular culture from music to television shows.[2] It's the first sequel ever included in the BFI Film Classics series. And – something of an aside but nevertheless an important feature of my analysis throughout this book – I love every second of this dark, messy, glorious film. Full of

The icy snowscapes of Hoth are visible in the promotional poster for *The Empire Strikes Back*, 1980

unexpected twists and turns (which might depend on both your age and ability to avoid forty-year-old spoilers), *Empire* propels viewers into fantastical worlds with evocative textures. There are the crystalline snowscapes of besieged ice-planet Hoth; the murky, twilight swamps of the deluged Dagobah; and the magnificence of the sun-speckled art deco city sitting high in the dusky atmosphere above Bespin. There are unexpected heroes, with a white woman, a Black man, and a cast of aliens and droids leading a rebellion against the evil Empire. Fantastical visual effects send asteroids spinning towards the screen. It is a film that continues to entrance and excite me even after countless viewings over close to three decades.

But what is perhaps surprising, especially given *Empire*'s prominence in popular culture, is that it tends to be neglected in serious critical and scholarly writing about Star Wars. Prior academic work has focused on the saga's industrial contexts, its fandom and remediation, and in some cases, textual analysis of the movies and other screen media.[3] Possibly as a result of the franchise's commercial success and mass appeal, it hasn't received the kind of archival investigation that tends to elevate discussions about other major cinematic texts (for example, the Bond franchise). Consequently, this book maps *Empire*'s social and political history, and focuses on the US and the UK as the two powers most heavily involved in the film's production. Over the next six chapters, I excavate the connections between *Empire* and its cultural contexts over the course of its lifetime, beginning with its genesis in November 1977 and ending with its classic status in the present day. In doing so, I delve into archives in LA and London, looking at the distributor's market research, as well as scribbled continuity sketches in homemade folders. I scour Lucasfilm trade publications to read between the lines of carefully constructed narratives of public record. I sort through stacks of digital and paper articles from the trade and daily press for reviews, news reports, and *Empire*-themed features. By drawing together the ephemeral traces of *Empire*'s production, exhibition, and ongoing reception, I propose a new and historically oriented direction of travel for critical writing about Star Wars. It is a film that has touched people's imaginations and daily lives through shared cultural reference points for over forty years; now, my aim is to make its past tangible to both new and nostalgic viewers alike. It may have been a long time ago, but by recovering and discussing its material history, *The Empire Strikes Back* doesn't have to feel so far away.

Weaving back and forth between my primary archival sources and broader histories of the 1970s and 1980s, I argue that *Empire* is a film about disruption. From its off-piste production to the oblique shapes and diagonal perspectives of its design, it's a film that disturbs the certainty of the status quo. Where *Star Wars* relies on stillness and stability, with static cameras and ships moving across screens in straight lines, *Empire* throws everything up in the air and leaves viewers guessing as to how it will all fall down. Characters bounce around inside ships; unstable landscapes tremble; cameras pan, tilt, and track. Off-screen, the film's journey to release navigated the Cold War and the 1978–9 Winter of Discontent, which saw trade unions in conflict with the UK government about pay and working conditions across sectors that impacted the film industries. *Empire* emerged amid furious debates about equality for women and people of colour, which resonated both in front of and behind the camera. And, following a chaotic production beset by fire, avalanches, and personal disputes, the film appeared in 1980 in an increasingly conservative political environment. Thus, this book addresses a broad range of possibly unexpected but nevertheless interconnected topics. There is militarism, trade unionism, and national identity; feminism, Black Power, and queer politics; colonialism and climate change; and the rise of New Hollywood. No matter what the angle, *Empire* is a turbulent film with a history rocked by conflict.

My perspective on the movie is informed by a particular set of experiences, too. I am a white, queer, cis, left-wing, feminist film historian and cultural critic. I am a trade unionist. I am also a lifelong Star Wars fan. As a child, I enjoyed the contentious *Ewoks*, which are often disparaged by adult fans (I still do enjoy them, really, and know all of their names). I am the kind of person who ordinarily doesn't get to write about Star Wars because even though I have the privilege of whiteness, I am not a man. But even as I question *Empire* and its politics, I maintain a love for the film and the franchise, which are inscribed in every word of this book. It is possible to occupy two positions at once and we are all, like our cultural artefacts, complicated and contradictory. Gregory E. Rutledge's work is exemplary here in laying out the challenges he faces as a Black scholar writing about racism in the Star Wars movies, even as he remains a fan.[4] And it is important for all of us, where we can, to acknowledge our biases if we are going to make meaningful contributions to the world-building process of writing about the past.[5] Consequently, I draw on Kimberlé Crenshaw's argument that society is built on intersecting oppressions such as gender, race, and class to help unpick how narratives about *Empire* have been shaped by subjective biases that underpin fandom of, and scholarship and criticism about, the film.[6] History, I argue, does not look the same either at or for all of us.

I therefore write this book from my position as under-represented in authorship about and in the fandom of Star Wars (as a queer woman), while also recognizing the privilege manifest

Luke hangs upside down in the wampa cave on Hoth; a low-angle shot and canted frame puts everything at odd angles as Han fixes the *Millennium Falcon* at the Rebels' Echo Base; Leia is destabilized by a tremor inside the exogorth

in my identity as an academic and critic who is white, cisgender, and non-disabled. It is my hope that writing this book will have three outcomes: first, that it will speak to other viewers who feel left out of Star Wars narratives.[7] Second, that people traditionally centred in writing about the franchise and its fandom will read the work with both generosity and curiosity and try to see from another point of view. And third, that it will create space for readers more marginalized than myself to respond to, build upon, challenge, or improve my arguments from their various subject positions. As bell hooks suggests, 'it is only as we collectively change the way we look at ourselves and the world that we can change how we are seen'.[8] Consequently, my small act of rebellion in this book is to resist oft-repeated claims about George Lucas and auteurism.[9] Instead, I focus on stories about the collective endeavours of film-makers and viewers so that others can more easily see and write about themselves in Star Wars criticism.

The following six chapters are organized chronologically to correspond with the life of the film. Chapter 1 offers an overview of the Star Wars franchise and *Empire*'s position within it, while also addressing its historical context. In Chapter 2, I explore the challenges of the film's production history. Chapter 3 is the soul of the book; here, I offer an analysis of *Empire* that draws together all of the book's historical and thematic concerns. Chapters 4 and 5 investigate the film's exhibition and reception among viewers and reviewers, while also considering the ruptures that the film generated in distribution models and criticism. And finally, in Chapter 6, I conclude by interrogating how the second-ranking box-office entry of the original trilogy, which was met with critical ambivalence and cynicism, became audiences' favourite Star Wars film. Referring to scholarship on taste, and thinking also about perceptions of the prequel and sequel films, I consider what *Empire* tells us about the changing status of entertainment franchises in popular culture.

The Empire Strikes Back, then, is a restless and uneasy movie that is full of contradictions and subject to shifting interpretations over the course of its history. My ambition in writing about the film has always been (if you will excuse the paraphrasing) to light sparks that stoke fires that broaden conversations about the film, its creators, and the diverse community of fans and viewers that continue to give the saga life.[10] And it is fitting, I feel, that my narrative should seek to disturb narratives about Star Wars. As another ephemeral presence in *Empire*'s afterlife, this book, too, will contribute to the film's ongoing, if ever-changing, history of disruption and resistance.

1 Creating an Empire

Star Wars is a global cultural phenomenon that has colonized cultural landscapes around the world. Referenced and remediated in literature, television shows, and other films, there are numerous paratexts (that is, other print and screen media that expand on the cinematic narratives), as well as vast merchandising lines and fan-created media. The saturation of everyday life with Star Wars dialogue, characters, and philosophies is so great that following a wave of census returns listing 'Jedi' as a religion in 2001 and 2011, the UK Charity Commission was forced to determine whether it was an official faith.[11] Since 2012, the Walt Disney Company's acquisition of the Star Wars canon, along with the Lucasfilm studio and its visual effects division Industrial Light and Magic (ILM), has helped create new generations of fans and ensure the continuing relevance of a vast media empire.[12]

But how did Star Wars come to acquire cultural capital? What was *Empire*'s role in the saga? And how did the tumultuous conditions of Hollywood and beyond inform *Empire*'s production and aesthetic? Paying attention to the generic conventions of *Star Wars* as well as its tentative connections to New Hollywood cinema, in this chapter I outline how *Empire* is situated in broader histories of film-making and both domestic and international politics. Arguing that the foundations of *Empire* were rooted in the cultural anxieties of the late 1970s, this chapter provides a framework for reading the themes and historical narratives that shape the rest of the book.

New Hollywood; new hope?
A long time ago, in a galaxy far, far away, *Star Wars* burst onto cinema screens and gathered a cult-like following among viewers,

who repeatedly returned to theatres to watch Princess Leia Organa (Carrie Fisher), Luke Skywalker (Mark Hamill), and Han Solo (Harrison Ford) battle against the villainous Darth Vader (voiced by James Earl Jones and performed by David Prowse). The film follows the Rebel Alliance and the Jedi – who defer to the Light Side of the mystical Force – as they fight the Empire and its Dark, Sith overlords. Based on the desert planet Tatooine, moisture farmer Luke intercepts a call for help from Leia via two droids (Kenny Baker's Artoo Detoo and Anthony Daniels' See Threepio). When Luke tracks down the message's intended recipient, a reclusive Jedi knight called Obi-Wan Kenobi (Alec Guinness), he and his new mentor begin a quest to rescue Leia and fight Vader's tyranny. Teaming up with bounty hunter Han and his shaggy-haired companion Chewbacca (or Chewie; Peter Mayhew), the accidental rebels face Vader and his menace of stormtroopers on the Death Star, a moon-like, weaponized space station. Luke eventually destroys the Death Star, and the film ends with Leia rewarding the Rebels at a ceremonial celebration. Vader, meanwhile, has a more ambiguous ending; he vanishes into space, overcome but not yet defeated.

A science-fiction space opera that recalls the 1936 serial adventures of *Flash Gordon*, as well as Greek myth and Arthurian legend, *Star Wars* and its prequels and sequels defy straightforward generic convention.[13] Indeed, scholars have long commented on the 'hybridity and fluidity' of science-fiction cinema, and have described Star Wars as both fantasy and a western.[14] There are romantic elements, too, with a love triangle between Han, Leia, and Luke. As critic Carol A. Crotta noted somewhat cynically in 1980, *Star Wars* was guilty of 'picking through genres like a shopping-bag lady through trash bins'.[15] Yet as scholar Christine Cornea argues, generic hybridity is crucial to the mass appeal of blockbuster cinema, and so the film navigates a range of registers that offer viewers a variety of modes through which to interpret the story.[16]

Alongside its playful engagement with genre, the movie also attracted viewers thanks to its explosive visual effects, which include a planet disintegrating into dust under laser fire and ships careening across star-flecked space. The technical artistry was down to visual effects teams at ILM under the direction of George Lucas, who with producer Gary Kurtz made the movie outside the confines of studio control. As Tara Lomax notes, 'since graduating from film school, Lucas has openly expressed distrust and cynicism towards the unchecked authority of the Hollywood studio system'.[17] His suspicions about studio practices were in keeping with his negative experiences on previous film edits and with his status as what Clyde Taylor calls 'one of the "movie brats" who ushered in "New Hollywood"'.[18] Since the mid-1960s, New Hollywood directors such as Francis Ford Coppola and Martin Scorsese had gained authorial power by eschewing studio finance in favour of independent production, and Lucas was an established figure in their set thanks to his work on *THX1138* (1971).[19] Certainly, in interviews, Lucas tended to cast himself as a plucky outsider with New Hollywood spirit, while on-screen, critics read the Rebel Alliance as freedom fighters, Vietnamese forces – or even New Hollywood film-makers – fighting the colonialist US government or the dogma of the studio system.

The blockbuster aesthetics of *Star Wars* nevertheless represent a departure from the usual tropes of New Hollywood's art-house style and its backlash against traditional film-making practices. And, as Peter Krämer suggests, in creating the behemoth Star Wars brand, Lucas merely established an alternative to the studio order of capitalist white patriarchy via merchandise.[20] For alongside a tie-in line of *Star Wars* toys manufactured by Kenner that quickly sold out in 1977, the *Los Angeles Times* listed a range of other consumables, including 'masks and costumes, t-shirts, lunch boxes, toothbrushes, posters, books, comics, bubble-gum cards, record albums, tapes and almost anything that might sell if it is tied to the box-office smash'.[21] The effect of the sales strategy was twofold. On the one hand, the commercial triumph of Star Wars via merchandise sales boosted revenue for Lucasfilm and its corporate partners. On the other, it provided significant resources to help the firm maintain authorial

The Kenner Toys *Star Wars* line sold out so quickly that the company issued empty boxes with gift certificates, c. 1977 (Courtesy of Kenner Toys and Lucasfilm)

control over what would soon become a multi-film franchise that was for the most part un-reliant on the studio system.

Consequently, in February 1978 Lucas announced that a sequel would enter production, and he confidently reported that the saga would incorporate nine films of which *Star Wars* was the fourth part.[22] However, the franchise's future was far from certain, and production on *The Empire Strikes Back* went over schedule and over budget.[23] Its box-office success was not guaranteed, either, with Lucasfilm marketing consultant Ashley Boone arguing that audiences had to be 'reconvinced' by a sequel.[24] Thus, in the run-up to *Empire*'s release, distributor Twentieth Century-Fox ran a campaign that saturated the media with TV spots, cast interviews, the early release of the soundtrack, radio advertising, and, of course, more merchandise.[25] Nothing about *Empire*'s success was left to chance.

The Empire attacks

In June 1980, a little over a month after opening in theatres, *The Empire Strikes Back* had secured 'the second largest weekend total of any new picture in film history', collecting $10,840,307 in box-office revenue from 823 US theatres.[26] Furthermore, the distributor expected it to exceed $50,000,000 'after only one week of wide release across the country'. Revenue, announced Twentieth Century-Fox, 'is running consistently higher than *Star Wars*'. While it never eclipsed the sales figures of *Star Wars* and remains behind Episode IV in adjusted box-office terms, *Empire* was a financial success and received positive audience responses.[27]

In the film, the Rebels have established a base on the ice planet Hoth, where they are tracked, attacked, and forced to flee by invading Imperial forces with giant mechanical 'Walkers', or AT-ATs. The protagonists take diverging paths: Luke travels to Dagobah to complete his Jedi training with Yoda (Frank Oz), a small, 900-year-old alien creature. Meanwhile, Leia, Han, Chewie, and Threepio hide out in an asteroid field before travelling to Bespin's Cloud City to seek protection from Lando Calrissian (Billy Dee Williams). They are attempting to evade Darth Vader and the Emperor (voiced by Clive Revill and played by Marjorie Eaton), who both fear Luke's increasing power. However, on reaching Bespin the Rebels walk into a trap, for Vader has blackmailed Lando into giving up their whereabouts in exchange for Cloud City's safety. Luke, sensing his friends are in trouble, defies Yoda and Obi-Wan's advice (his mentor reappears as a Force ghost) and journeys to Bespin. He is too late to save Han, who is frozen in carbonite and handed to bounty hunter Boba Fett (Jeremy Bulloch) for delivery to crime lord Jabba the Hutt. Luke and Vader then battle in a lightsaber duel: Vader cuts off Luke's hand, and in the film's plot twist, reveals that he is Luke's father. Barely alive after his rejection of Vader's entreaties to join the Dark Side, Luke is rescued by Leia, Lando, Chewie, and the droids. Disheartened but not yet defeated, they set off to rescue Han.

With the Rebels' victory uncertain, *Empire*'s narrative ambiguity resists a definite conclusion. Directed by Irvin Kershner, who was known for the character-driven and spectacularly camp *The Eyes of Laura Mars* (1978), *Empire* further destabilizes the uniformity of classical cinema with its restless cinematography and canted framing.[28] Whereas *Star Wars* works on geometric planes along x, y, and z (width, height, and depth) axes – all right angles and static cinematography – *Empire* introduces anxiety-inducing diagonal planes, or 'space diagonals' that use asymmetry to create visual tension. Indeed, when Carrie Fisher said of the film, 'sure, it's a fairy tale, just like the first, but it has an additional dimension', she could have been referring to characterization or the film's aesthetics.[29] Moreover, the film's bolder, darker colour palette (which recalls the melodramas of Powell and Pressburger or Douglas Sirk), and eerie invocation of a ghostly Vader in the Dagobah gloom, introduce elements of camp, Gothic horror to the saga.[30] Writing in *The Washington Post*, Gary Arnold proposed that the 'deliberately unresolved sequel […] [is] aligning the story in a powerful, sinister new direction, full of dreadful implications for the original movie and the sequels ahead'.[31] And with myriad social and political upheavals affecting both the US and the UK in 1980, *Empire*'s darker themes spoke to potential horrors occurring off-screen as well as on it.

Dark times

The moral and narrative uncertainty of *Empire* emerged from and into a cultural maelstrom of paranoia and change: alongside escalations in the Cold War and crises in living standards, Clyde Taylor points to economic anxieties which caused a 'tremor in confidence' in the 'contradictions of advanced capitalism'.[32] Certainly, the film is full of visual tremors. The cast bounce around the screen and rock back and forth as the Rebels weave between incoming asteroids in the *Millennium Falcon*, and the earth moves beneath them inside the mouth of a monstrous exogorth. Indeed, David S. Meyer refers to *Empire* as a film of 'disarray' and suggests that it speaks to the 'political upheaval' that led to President Carter losing to Ronald Reagan in the presidential election of November 1980.[33] In the UK, where the film's studio shoot took place, there was similar political turbulence. Stuart Hall, writing in 1979, acknowledged the 'swing to the Right' that had been gaining 'dynamic and momentum' since the late 1960s and preceded Margaret Thatcher's Conservative Party winning an election held during *Empire*'s production.[34] The film thus emerged amid upheaval and disturbance.

In his work on the original trilogy films in 1986, Robin Wood argued that increasingly right-wing politics at the turn of the 1980s brought about a desire for films such as *Star Wars* and *Empire* that offered 'the comforting nostalgia for the childish [and the] repetitive pleasure of comic strip and serial'.[35] In the aftermath of Vietnam and Watergate, he proposed that 'reassurance is the keynote'.[36] Later, writing in 1993, Ed Guerrero described Star Wars as 'a white versus Black allegory that celebrated the recovery of patriarchy and a technological militarism', that, as a product of the corporatized blockbuster genre, relied on repetition rather than experimentation.[37] Yet while *Empire* is a sequel that offers repetitive aesthetic pleasure by returning viewers to a familiar galaxy (a galaxy that, as Taylor suggests, is also nostalgic for an imagined white nation free from the impact of, say, the civil rights movement or Windrush) it does not provide the stability of narrative repetition.[38] There are, of course, callbacks, such as Leia repeating Han's *Star Wars* line 'I have a bad feeling about this'. But the plot, which resists resolution and opens up the possibility of failure for the Rebels, instead works to make viewers *un*comfortable.

Off-screen, there were other major cultural anxieties, too. The production was challenged by inflation and rising oil prices that affected the cost of plastic props and costumes.[39] And the Cold War instilled fears about nuclear attacks, surveillance, and double agents that can be traced through Star Wars in the destruction of the Death Star in Episode IV, and the Imperial droid that seeks out the Rebels on Hoth in Episode V.[40] On a related note, Vivian Sobchack's work on science-fiction cinema analyses how movies from the Cold War period 'are filled with dystopian despair. Rather than figuring children (and through "conceiving" a future), the films mark the socially necessary or externally imposed absence of children'.[41] There are, of course, no visible children in the nuclear-age *Star Wars* or *The Empire Strikes Back*. Additionally, there were widespread social concerns about the environment, with the daily press reporting the effects of pollutants, carbon emissions, and global warming.[42] Throughout *Empire*, even the morally superior Rebels are in conflict with the hostile landscapes that they invade and inhabit, from the deathly cold of Hoth to the enraged exogorth that Han shoots with his blaster. The shaky ground and tremulous atmosphere that pervade the film are not only references to the challenging conditions brought about by changing governments, but also growing anxieties about the durability of Earth itself.

Finally, the domestic affairs of the US and the UK had a profound impact on *Empire*'s production and aesthetics. Writing about the US context (it is worth noting that people in the UK faced similar, but differently realized, injustices), Adilifu Nama describes how 'race relations were a political tinderbox about to explode'.[43] Thus, *Empire*'s introduction of Black character Lando represents the uncertain status of African American citizens in the late 1970s, as it 'occurs at a time when affirmative action as a racial remedy is fuelling a national debate about American meritocracy and the idea of a colour-blind society'.[44] And, although mainstream second-wave feminist discourse tended to prioritize white, middle-class women and overlook the important work of women of colour – tellingly, there are no women of colour in *Empire* at all – in the run up to *Empire*'s release there were continuing battles over women's rights. Ironically, while Leia's representation as a science-fiction heroine who commands a spaceship has long been praised by feminist viewers for its depiction of women's abilities, in 1980 no American female astronauts had travelled to space.[45] In the film, Leia has significantly more screen time than in *Star Wars* and demonstrates both leadership and autonomy; Carolyn Cocca contends that Leia 'showed that women could be leaders [...] that courage and conviction were not only male traits but human traits'.[46] Nevertheless, she also acknowledges Leia's exceptional status as the sole woman protagonist: not all women are capable, only Leia. The same is true for Lando as an exceptional Black man, too.

On both sides of the Atlantic, then, *Empire*'s film-makers were working in a period of cultural, political, and economic instability, in which the centrist and left-wing policies of the US Democrats and UK Labour were threatened or overturned by the increasing power of newly elected right-wing Republican and Conservative governments. Whatever the individual politics of the creative talent involved in making *Empire*, they faced anxieties ranging from the Cold War and climate change to gender and racial inequalities. Throughout the rest of this book, I argue that such tensions simmered below and bubbled across the surface of the film, as well as manifesting in its production and reception.

2 In Production

From blizzards and fires to technical challenges, production on *The Empire Strikes Back* was notoriously disruptive and disrupted. Many reports detailed the hardships that the film-makers faced between 1978 and the film's release in 1980. Today, most histories of the production are official, Lucasfilm commissioned sources, with J. W. Rinzler's *The Making of The Empire Strikes Back* offering a thorough and in-depth investigation of the production cycle.[47] Taking a more meta perspective on the various extant production accounts, I read across a variety of primary and secondary materials (including interviews conducted with some crew members for this book) to interrogate how and why the film-makers knowingly represented *Empire*'s production as chaotic. According to both Lucasfilm and press reports, the film was a feat of ingenuity that proved the production team's commitment to serving Star Wars fans; *Empire* was an accomplishment seemingly on a par with polar exploration made by the best and most devoted artists. In the spirit of New Hollywood independence from which it emerged, Episode V was the underdog movie made against the odds – despite being the sequel to the highest grossing film of all time.

In exploring *Empire*'s production, I imagine its history as similar to the composite special effects shots that make up so much of the film. Within the sources there are layer upon layer of fact, bias, official narrative, and personal storytelling that are all compiled together to create one big picture. Consequently, I excavate the constituent parts of the production's composition and frame them with historical context. There are three layers to this chapter: first there are the foregrounded features, such as the visible disruptions to the film-making process that the crew openly discussed in press reports. Next come the contingent elements, which pertain to disruptions caused by militarism, trade unionism, and the cultural differences between the US and UK. Finally, I discuss the backgrounded issues, such as the marginalized and often erased labour of women on the shoot.

Foreground features

In the current cultural environment, reports about interpersonal adversity, budget concerns, and delays to a film shoot would likely prompt press reports concerned about a movie's quality and box-office performance.[48] Yet in *Empire*'s case, narratives of disruption contributed to its mystique. The technical challenges facing the crew commenced with principal photography on 5 March 1979.[49] Arriving at Finse, Norway, to shoot the snowy exterior sequences located on Hoth, the cast and crew were cut off for several days by avalanches on the railway line. Throughout the shoot, the 'arctic survival camp' that housed them was buried by snow, and blizzards frequently interrupted filming.[50] To compound their problems, location second-unit director Peter MacDonald and assistant cameraman Mike Brewster recall that they could only access the rushes (the unedited footage from the shoot) with four days' delay because they had no facilities to develop the film stock in the 'hostile' glacial environment.[51] Director Irvin Kershner explained: 'It got to be 26 degrees below zero [...] The camera equipment had to be winterized with special lightweight oil in the gears to stop them freezing up [...] You had to handle the film carefully because it becomes very brittle and cracks.'[52] Based at the same Norwegian location as Captain Scott when he trained his teams for Antarctic expeditions in the 1910s, *Empire*'s production took on the tone of a *Boys' Own* adventure story. As such, the creative talent's commitment in the face of physical hardship suggested that they would do anything to serve the eager fans of *Star Wars*.

Reports about the studio shoot at Elstree in London told a similar story of disruption. Before work on *Empire* began, the studio lost an entire stage when a fire broke out on the set of *The Shining*, which delayed the Star Wars team and restricted the available space.[53]

The vast set of the *Millennium Falcon* is visible at Elstree, 1979

When the shoot did get underway, the enormous production employed a team of over ninety people who worked six or seven days per week 'for many, many months' across five stages.[54] One specially built space was the largest sound stage in the world. But even that was not large enough to accommodate the life-size *Millennium Falcon* (also known as the *Falcon*) or the Dagobah swamp – it required a further expansion and a crane to lift off a section of the roof.[55] Recalling his time on the shoot, Kershner said that, 'I would often walk onto a set that I had never seen before, and the paint was still wet, because they had painted all night'.[56] Speaking to me in an interview, Second Assistant Cameraman Madelyn Most (one of the few women on set) recounted how the paint and aerosols used to create the glittering snow of the Rebel's Echo Base would heat up under the studio lights and affect the crew's breathing.[57] Most describes other challenges, too, such as getting the lens 'acclimated to the steam' to avoid condensation during Luke and Vader's duel, and matching frames of the physical film on a Movieola to 'big walls of storyboards […] perfectly by eye' ready for the special effects departments to take over.[58]

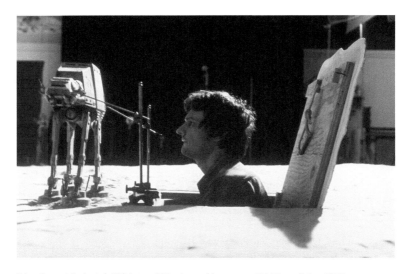

John Berg at Industrial Light and Magic working on an AT-AT model, c. 1979

Once the crew completed the live-action sequences, the special visual effects teams at ILM worked up to twelve hours per day, six days per week in California to complete the film.[59] Using an Apple II computer and a new optical printer, the team worked in a specially designed environment featuring filtered air with temperature and humidity control to create multilayered composite images.[60] Scenes such as those on Hoth required more advanced and innovative work than *Star Wars* as the artists rendered multiple elements together. A single frame could contain live-action footage of the snowspeeders and actors; animated model Walkers; animated flak, lasers, and explosions; and either mattes (painted backgrounds) or live-action aerial footage. In total, the ILM team composited 415 shots for *Empire* in a year.[61] The sound design also required extensive labour and posed numerous challenges. In a 1994 interview, Mark Hamill suggested that up to 90 per cent of the dialogue was dubbed, referring to the 'unreality' of the shooting experience owing to the ambient noise of robotic props and characters

A scene on Hoth that composited live-action studio footage, a location shot, and stop-motion AT-ATs all in the same frame

on set.[62] Thus, from start to finish, Lucasfilm employees reported a production beset by technological and physical challenges that in being overcome represented a sizeable achievement on behalf of fans.

Furthermore, official histories of the franchise propose that the teams at both Elstree and ILM changed the direction of cinema aesthetics by overturning classical film-making traditions. Certainly, Julie Turnock's research indicates that there were overlaps between 'experimental artist-filmmakers and special effects technicians' such as visual effects supervisor Richard Edlund.[63] Yet Turnock also suggests that Lucas prevented artists from incorporating avant-garde elements that deviated from his conservative vision of Star Wars.[64] Moreover, interviews with the special effects team often reveal that while they were keen to disrupt traditional modes of film-making, they were indebted to classical techniques. For example, Edlund states in multiple interviews that he was reliant on the past: he sought out technicians from the defunct studio effects departments of the 1950s for advice and used archival materials to help build high-speed VistaVision cameras for the *Empire* shoot.[65] Similarly, matte painter Harrison Ellinshaw argued that, 'I don't think anything we did on *The Empire Strikes Back* could be called startlingly innovative […] I think everything we do today is still at the most, new applications of old ideas'.[66] The effects team's increasing reliance on computers was transformative and did represent a form of disruption to analogue models of film-making. However, as Edlund and Ellinshaw's testimonies suggest, official accounts of the movie sometimes diverged from those of the film-makers.

Contingent elements

Conflict abounds through *Empire*'s history, with the broader destabilizing effects of industrial and national politics also shaping the production, particularly with regard to its military links and the different labour contexts of its US and UK teams. That a franchise called 'Star Wars' should have material connections to the military (with the suggestion of armed conflict literally advertised by its title) is unsurprising. Indeed, according to Friedrich Kittler, the history of media technologies has *always* been militaristic, with the transport of celluloid through a projector reliant on the same mechanisms designed for automatic machine guns.[67] He also argues that owing to technological similarities and the ability of film-makers to turn war into spectacle, 'the entertainment industry is, in any conceivable sense of the word, an abuse of army equipment'.[68] While Kittler's argument applies to all feature films, not just those in the Star Wars franchise, *Empire* has a materially military-based production history that further embeds the film in the landscape of war.

The creative team's own military experiences, for example, are emphasized throughout the movie's publicity. Brian Johnson, the special visual effects lead, was 'a camera assistant in the British Film Studios before joining the Royal Air Force for two years, during which time he worked on instrument landing systems'.[69] Reporter John May's account of the film also played up artist Ralph McQuarrie's military background, recounting his twenty years' experience as a technical illustrator for military-adjacent aircraft companies, including Boeing.[70] Additionally, Lucasfilm also invoked associations with the military or outsourced the creation of props and technical elements to national armed forces. Finse was the site of British military polar training, and the location team took advice from NATO to keep their gear working in the cold Norwegian climate.[71] The helicopter used by the crew there for aerial shots was a British RAF aircraft (the Aerospatiale Lama 315B), which owing to its foreign origin required permissions from the Norwegian military.[72] The bacta tank that viewers see in the medical bay on Hoth – containing 400 gallons of chlorinated water, and at over seven feet high 'the largest of its kind ever made' – was constructed by British Aerospace, a munitions and defence manufacturer now recognizable as BAE Systems.[73] And, when recording the 1,000 new sounds that populated the film, Ben Burtt 'crawled into foxholes' with his tape recorder at a missile base and was shot at by the artillery.[74] Thus, publicity for the film makes clear the movie's proximity to actual conflict. In doing so, the narrative proves the creative team's professionalism and commitment to the *Empire* production while also suggesting that the film has a degree of authenticity unusual for a family-friendly blockbuster – *Empire* is serious about war.

The military evocations also speak to broader cultural disturbances. For by insinuating that the armed forces and their suppliers' involvement in the Star Wars franchise made the film more authentic, the film-makers simultaneously indicated that *Empire* was a show of US and UK military power. That the Americans and British could produce a technologically innovative blockbuster film at the height of the Cold War that relied on support from firms such as British Aerospace demonstrated the nations' soft power (that is, cultural influence) as well as financial and military resources. It therefore situates *Empire* within the military-industrial complex, which is an alliance between military forces and the defence industries that enable them.[75] Furthermore, the film's production was affected by the 1979 energy crisis, which saw oil prices surge in the wake of the Iranian Revolution. Acknowledging that *Empire* cost $20 million dollars more to make than *Star Wars*, producer Gary Kurtz blamed energy price inflation. He said that, 'we used a lot of set-dressing materials based on plastics – petroleum-based products – and the price of those has gone up astronomically. Pieces of pipe and tubing now cost around three or four times what they cost three years ago'.[76] The White Horse Toy Company's manufacture of lightweight Artoo units demonstrates the film's reliance on plastics: the units used 'fibreglass, thermoplastic and aluminium moulded into about 200 separate parts and […] a rigid polyurethane inner skin'.[77] While the film's military antecedents helped promote the sequel as a serious and politically significant endeavour, global conflict simultaneously disrupted the production.

Of course, in military contexts the US and the UK were self-professed allies. But that alliance did not necessarily extend to other aspects of their identities. Consequently, a second element of cultural disturbance appears within histories of *Empire*'s production that refers to the conflicting needs of the UK-based Elstree team, who are represented in Lucasfilm accounts as haphazard, and the US-based ILM, who are more professional. For instance, the over-schedule Elstree shoot seemed to be caused by a combination of Kershner's European art-house sensibility and indecision, and the British team's clearly defined working hours. Indeed, the call sheets advertise regular morning and afternoon breaks and the importance of workers recording their hours on time sheets.[78] In contrast, staff at ILM reportedly worked twelve-hour shifts that rotated night and day to enable twenty-four-hour production. Yet the slower speed of production in the UK was probably not a sign of unprofessionalism but rather a result of hard-won workers' rights brought about by both a trade unionist ethos under a Labour government and the pro-union Film Producers' Association.[79] That the shoot got underway roughly on schedule was fortunate in itself. As Alan Arnold notes, the Elstree filming occurred 'despite Britain's general industrial gloom' in which 'strikes had shut down half the economy in what was being called "the Winter of Discontent"'.[80]

In addition, the UK film industry had long relied on US funding for domestic productions. Sian Barber describes British film-makers' uneasiness about the relationship between the two nations, with US finances propping up UK cinema while simultaneously benefitting from tax deductions that enriched the Hollywood studios.[81] In an interview, Kurtz noted that he 'perceived some hostility' in the UK, as some people 'felt that we had come to England and used its resources and taken all the money away'.[82] He was keen to assure everyone that Lucasfilm was spending $15 million on the new production, and that profits would be reinvested in the UK economy by the distributor in future. However, Lucasfilm's own presentation of its relationship with its transatlantic ally served to reinforce the US's superior status. The *Empire* pressbook announcing the new sound stage built at Elstree – 'an important new facility for the film industry in Britain' – implied that Lucasfilm was once again professionalizing its UK colleagues.[83] That the relationship between Lucasfilm, ILM, and Elstree continued on Episode VI indicates that the franchise did, in meaningful ways, help bridge national and cultural gaps. Nevertheless, the publicity materials suggest that even if inadvertently, the production was beset by division and difference.

Backgrounded issues

In the final section of this chapter, I turn my attention to a form of division rampant in both the film industry in general and *Empire* in particular: the marginalization of women in production roles. Here, I focus on women's contributions, which tend to be erased from historical accounts by patriarchal record keeping and historiography – indeed, while there are thirty-five women listed in the film's credits, only screenwriter Leigh Brackett is afforded serious discussion in most production narratives.[84] My decision is not designed to ignore race or erase people who are gender queer; within the scope of this book, women's involvement in the production is, in general, more readily traceable than other elements of identity owing to names providing *likely* indicators of gender.[85] As such, I begin to uncover women's work on *Empire* by situating their contributions in broader histories of gender and labour that disrupt male-centric narratives about the movie. For besides Carrie Fisher's Princess Leia, women are notably underrepresented in

Marjorie Eaton appears as the face of the Emperor

The Empire Strikes Back. Stephanie English speaks one line at
the rebel base on Hoth; Cathy Munro appears as the masked and
male bounty hunter Zuckuss; Marjorie Eaton provides the face of
another male character, the mysterious Emperor. Behind the camera,
women did not fare well either.[86]

In the late 1970s, mainstream and white-oriented second-wave
feminism and the male-oriented Black Power movement (which was
in decline) were two of the dominant modes of resistance to white
patriarchy. Yet in spite of vocal and organized support for equality in
US and UK cultures, *Empire* did not provide equal opportunities, and
only two women receive substantial attention in its contemporary
production histories. The first is Leigh Brackett, the science fiction
and hard-boiled crime novelist and screenwriter who wrote the
original *Empire* script and sadly died of cancer following completion
of the first draft. Lucasfilm paid Brackett 'a flat-fee of $50,000
dollars and the typist $500 for the script' (given the gendered history
of typewriting, the typist was, no doubt, a woman whose labour was
uncredited).[87] Brackett herself gets short shrift in Rinzler's write-up
of script development, which denigrates her for clunky dialogue
and outdated ideas.[88] Yet her original draft is foundational to the
shooting script's structure and character development. Luke grows

up during his Jedi training, and Leia and Han's screwball-comedy dialogue is evident, although in Brackett's script their interactions tend to be gentle rather than aggressive. For instance, Leia smiles at Han on Hoth and says, 'I know you better than you know yourself'. 'A man always hates to hear a woman tell him that', he replies, 'it might just be true, and what a catastrophe that would be!'[89] In later editions of the script, Han's admission of women's power is erased and his exchanges with Leia become more brusque.

The most generous account of any woman's work on the film (for women do not get to tell their own stories) was provided by her male superior's intervention. Writing in trade journal *American Cinematographer* in a special issue about *Empire*'s production, aerial cinematographer Ronald C. Goodman drew deliberate attention to camera assistant Margaret Herron, who 'in addition to her normal camera duties, had the quite unique and difficult job of riding shotgun on the camera speed'.[90] As the helicopter banked and turned, 'Margaret's difficult task was to anticipate these g-force changes and maintain constant camera speed and, therefore, exposure'. Impressed by Herron's work, Goodman disrupted a narrative of exclusively male achievement, and his praise for

An example of the aerial photography that Margaret Herron contributed to filming in Norway

Herron makes the erasure of women's work in other accounts of the production more acute.

In her work on women in the UK's screen industries, Melanie Bell focuses on women's labour as Foley artists (a sound recording role). She notes that while women served as Foley artists, which necessitated working in pairs, productions only tended to credit them as 'sound effects editors'.[91] Until the mid-1980s, men denied women access to union membership and undermined the creativity of their female colleagues' work. Bell also notes that 'women's over-representation in the role [likely] contributed to its under-representation in film history'.[92] Examining the *Empire* credits is revealing: two women, Teresa Eckton and Bonnie Koehler, are listed as sound editors, with Joanna Cappuccilli, Nancy Jencks, and Laurel Ladevich as assistants. Yet none of the women, who were likely responsible for vital Foley work, have major profiles in official histories of the film; most references to sound in contemporary publicity materials credit Ben Burtt alone.[93]

Women's labour was undermined in other areas, too. In an ILM anecdote reported by Rinzler that points to a machismo workplace culture, executive Dick Gallegly fired two female administrative staff after they made joke purchases of furs and jewellery to show him up for approving documents without reading them.[94] Other women credited on the picture appear in roles that are stereotypically associated with female labour – for example, Barbara Ellis was the assistant film editor.[95] Even today, the gendered nature of work often leads to highly skilled positions such as editing (which on 35mm shoots bears a resemblance to the equally skilful, yet simultaneously feminized, activities of cloth cutting and sewing) being seen as women's roles in the patriarchal film industry. Nevertheless, there were women present in all areas of *Empire*'s creation: Kim Knowlton, Nina Saxon, and Diana Wilson were animators at ILM, and there were likely many uncredited women contributing to catering, cleaning, and secretarial roles that supported the production.

Across multiple aspects of its production, then, *Empire*'s creative genesis was one of disturbance. Promotional narratives about the film aimed to impress audiences with military authenticity and technical challenges while also referring obliquely to the Cold War, energy crisis, and national and gendered labour practices that simultaneously underpinned and destabilized the shoot. And, whether consciously or not, the film itself would inscribe the conflicts that informed its production in its on-screen aesthetics.

3 The Film

I can still remember the thrill of watching *The Empire Strikes Back* and realizing for the first time the magnitude of Darth Vader's paternal revelation. It was the early 1990s, and I was sitting very close to the edge of a large, heavy-set green sofa. The blinds in the window were drawn. The television by today's standards was small and the film was playing on VHS; probably, given our financial circumstances at the time, it was a cassette that my parents taped off the TV or borrowed from the library. I was about eight years old and my dad was reintroducing me to the Star Wars films during the school holidays. If memory serves, we watched all three films in quick succession, perhaps even that day.

I recall this story as a preface to my textual analysis of *Empire* to emphasize the highly personal connection that I – that all viewers – have with the film. Everyone has their own points of entry into the Star Wars galaxy that are informed by gender, race, class, age, geography, and so on (for example, as a result of my age and thanks to corporate theatrical distribution strategies, I haven't seen *Empire* in a cinema). Whether readers first saw the movie on its release in 1980 or on a tablet computer in 2019, their interpretations of the film are subjective and valid. In this chapter, I continue my own subjective exploration of the movie within a framework of disturbance that, like *Empire* itself, has five constituent parts. I discuss environments and climate change; the ideology of war; generational transformations; the gendered and racialized politics of rebellion; and queer villainy. The chapter is organized according to *Empire*'s own linear narrative – however, like the film, the interconnected themes and ideas necessitate some changes of direction along the way.

It's getting Hoth in here

From the opening paragraph of the opening crawl, *Empire* destabilizes its Rebel protagonists. Since the end of *Star Wars*, they have been 'driven from their hidden base' and 'pursued' by Imperial forces. They are uprooted and precarious, and the relative peace of the medal ceremony on Yavin 4 is gone. In analysing the movie's planetary and other terrains, I draw on Giuliana Bruno's enticement to think about cinema as spatial and to engage with its 'history and its inhabited, lived space'.[96] Throughout the film, the Rebels' resting places are temporary and the environments they inhabit are inhospitable, with tremors, vibrations, and monstrous creatures disturbing the equilibrium. Indeed, the environments and creatures that the Rebels encounter are so hostile that Darth Vader and the stormtroopers often pose less of an immediate threat to the protagonists' safety. On Hoth, for example, the cold temperatures are life-threatening to its visitors. As Luke surveys the white plains from the back of a tauntaun, on a reconnaissance mission with Han Solo, the already forbidding space is disturbed by an Imperial surveillance droid crash-landing nearby. Moments later, an off-screen attacker causes the tauntaun to buck and throw an off-balanced Luke to the ground, where he is mauled by a yeti-like wampa and dragged away.

Luke is dragged along the ground diagonally across the screen in a wampa attack on Hoth

As See Threepio announces, the odds of overnight survival outside of Echo Base are just 725 to 1.

Additionally, Dagobah is a humid swamp that renders human technology obsolete, with Luke's X-wing sinking into the murky waters and Artoo immobile in the wild terrain. The elegant Cloud City, meanwhile, relies on a complex architectural infrastructure that enables its citizens to live on gas planet Bespin. As Toby Neilson argues, weapons and environmental destruction in the Disney-era Star Wars films (for instance, the Starkiller Base exploding in the 2015 *The Force Awakens*) 'appear more like strange and dangerous weather than strange and dangerous technology'.[97] But strange and dangerous weather is apparent in *Empire*, too. As such, it is rooted in climate change discourse that was pervasive in the 1970s, with cultural anxieties about extreme weather conditions as a result of carbon emissions and other pollutants commonplace in the daily press. While the environmental movement had peaked prior to *Empire*'s release, the film's landscapes are plagued by ecological dysfunction. Its attentiveness to environmental disasters was likely influenced by director Irvin Kershner, who was a staunch advocate of vegetarianism and spiritual harmony between living things and their habitats.[98] As Alan Arnold notes, the film directs viewers 'toward

Han and Luke take shelter in the hostile climate of Hoth

assuming responsibility for oneself and one's environment'.[99] After all, it is Han who causes the exogorth inside the asteroid to turn on the Rebels when he shoots it with his blaster pistol; he is responsible for their imminent deaths, not the creature.

Alongside set design, *Empire*'s cinematography and visual effects also contribute to a general sense of destabilization, as the terrain of the first film is disrupted by a more mobile camera. Editor Paul Hirsch, who worked on both Episodes IV and V, described how 'in *Star Wars*, the camera hardly ever moved, therefore much of the film's energy was generated from editing. In this film [*Empire*] there are more camera movements and energy is generated without the need for such rapid cutting.'[100] Within the frame, too, characters and props are set at odds with their environments. On-screen space is consistently broken up in Echo Base by glass screens covered in swirling patterns that distort the faces of the Rebels in scenes with Leia and General Rieekan (Bruce Boa). Canted angles and diagonals also abound on the Dark Side: medium shots and close ups of officers that at first appear balanced are often slightly off-centre in their framing; Vader's chamber is a terrifying mouth-like structure with oblique teeth. In one high-angle shot aligned with the hem of Vader's cloak, the camera peers down on Imperial officers who are vulnerable under his authority. Everywhere there is visual uncertainty, and almost no one is safe in a galaxy threatened by human conflict.

Leia, Han, Chewie, and Threepio fare little better on the *Falcon*, which soars, loops, and rocks its crew back and forth, side to side, and up and down as they attempt to escape the Imperial TIE-fighters. Their tense dash through the asteroid field is a visual wonder. With the camera positioned behind the cast as they look out with trepidation at the huge rocks hurtling towards them, viewers are given their own point-of-view shot and effectively invited to inhabit the cockpit alongside the characters. The horizon is unstable and shifting, and the blasts and booms of lasers and asteroid impacts layered over John Williams' dynamic score increases the audiovisual anxiety. It is a choreographed

Glass screens covered in swirling patterns break up and distort the space of the
Rebels' Echo Base on Hoth; Vader emerges from his chamber, which is designed with
oblique teeth-like features

juxtaposition of harmony and discordance that represents the
tensions in *Empire* between the human need for survival and the
danger that humans inevitably create. Later, the Rebels' arrival on
Bespin besieges them with more uneasy-looking sets and camera
angles. Yet, there are moments of stability. Hiding on the side
of an Imperial cruiser, a canted angle shows Threepio, Chewie,
Leia, and Han in the *Millennium Falcon*. As the *Falcon* detaches
from the larger ship, the camera angle rights the characters along
x–y axes: unmoored from any gravitational force, the characters
are afforded an ironic moment of respite from movement along
what in geometric terms are known as space diagonals (the angles

Darth Vader's cloak sweeps above the Imperial officers; the Rebel crew of the *Millennium Falcon* in the asteroid field

between different faces or planes of a 3D object). No longer in conflict with the environment, the Rebels have a moment of peace.

The coldest of wars

Armed conflict, though, gives *Empire* its narrative impetus and the visual and sonic anxieties that pervade the screen speak to military and colonial violence. While critics have a range of theories about the politics of the original trilogy films, citing US hostilities against Vietnam and the Cold War as possible ideological frameworks (the battle on Hoth is literally a *cold war*), most agree that the movies are politically conservative.[101] Scholars support the argument

The crew of the *Millennium Falcon* are on a diagonal axis (note the blue light signifying danger as Han suggests they fly to Bespin) that is righted along an x–y axis as they float into space and relative safety

with evidence of the franchise's own cultural imperialism and whitewashing of historical source material.[102] For example, Gregory E. Rutledge discusses Williams' appropriation of Black jazz traditions in the score of the cantina scene in *Star Wars*.[103] Kevin J. Wetmore also proposes that the two opposing sides in the films are alike, as 'both the Rebellion and the Empire are fighting for the right of privileged white males to control the galaxy'.[104] Furthermore, Wetmore points out that indigenous and invaded groups like the Ewoks in *Return of the Jedi* support the Rebels, much like subaltern troops in the First and Second World Wars aided colonizing European forces. Given that in *Empire* the Rebel Alliance does not offer an explicit alternative system of governance to Imperial rule, the heroes and the villains operate from similar positions.

Where *Star Wars* created visual similarities between the Rebel and Imperial characters mostly through costuming (for example, Luke and Han disguise themselves as stormtroopers), *Empire* establishes aesthetic parallels between the sides in its lighting, colour grading, set design, and framing. Blue and red lights infuse the Rebellion's Echo Base and Vader's Imperial cruiser with an eerie glow; computer graphics and control panels are the same on both sides. That both colours filter both Rebel and Imperial spaces suggests not so much a tension between them as within each side itself: Vader faces insubordination and disagreements with the Emperor; Leia, Han, and Chewie face Lando's betrayal, and Luke disputes the best course of action with Yoda. All of their weapons sound the same, too, with Imperial and Rebel laser fire and blaster pistols indistinguishable (the film relies on the score to create audible differences between the warring factions). During the Battle of Hoth, the editing is disorienting and switches direction, making the viewer's position in the battle uncertain, and both sides are shot using canted frames. Visually disturbing oblique angles are embedded in both aesthetics as well, with doors, corridors, and windows from TIE-fighters to domestic space on Bespin sharing similar diagonal motifs. The

The Rebels lean over a control panel lit with red and blue lights; the Imperial control panels are lit in similar red and blue hues

blue of Luke's Light Side lightsaber is no longer a sure signifier of good, for blue lights also emanate from Echo Base before it collapses, and from the side-room where Threepio is attacked and dismantled on Bespin.

In the blue-red blaze of the galactic war, both sides are, at the mid-point of the original trilogy (and now the central film of the three trilogies) balanced in their opposition. That is not to suggest that the two sides are exactly the same. Rather, as David Seed argues about the Cold War, 'we encounter a principle of reversibility where characteristics attributed to one bloc mirror those of the other'.[105] Even though their alternative system of governance is unclear, the

The bridge of an AT-AT: the blaster fire and tilted framing looks the same from Imperial and Rebel point of views; Threepio stumbles into a blue-lit trap on Bespin

Rebels are fighting for freedom from Imperial rule and have a more inclusive, albeit patriarchal and white, social hierarchy. Nevertheless, in attempting to overthrow the Empire they do sometimes adopt its strategies. On Hoth, for instance, they are colonizers that use the land for its resources. The tauntaun do not seem to be an indigenous species (they die easily in the cold temperatures), and seen from Luke's point of view, the injury he causes the wampa is justified because it (a native creature on Hoth) attacked him (an invader). While the Rebels' technology is not as advanced – they are reliant on radio transmissions rather than moving-image surveillance, and their ships are fewer in number and not as well equipped – they continue to participate in and thus perpetuate a military-industrial complex that commoditizes conflict. And as Lando's double-agent status attests in another moment of Cold War-like politics within the film, everyone has their price. *Empire*'s effect then, is to embrace the ethical uncertainty of war and avoid telling neat fairy tales about good versus evil. It generates sympathy for the Rebel Alliance by positioning viewers in their emotional space and counter to the terror of an Empire that, like the alien threats that Susan Sontag describes in 1960s science fiction, is 'a regime of emotionlessness […] impersonality'.[106] Yet via its aesthetics and narrative of colonization, the film complicates the relationship between Skywalkers and Star Destroyers rather than resolving them.

From the Dark time to the Light

If the politics of the Dark Side and the Light are a grey area, *Empire*'s delineation between old and new is no less conflicted, with the film's temporality just as vital to the plot as its spatiality. In the film, as in *Star Wars*, it is the older generation of characters which notices that change is coming. 'There is a great disturbance in the Force', says the Emperor to Vader, who responds, 'I have felt it', with their exchange echoing Obi-Wan's line in Episode IV, 'I felt a great disturbance in the Force'. But whereas Obi-Wan senses a disruption caused by the Dark Side (the Empire is destroying Leia's home planet, Alderaan, using the Death Star), Vader and the Emperor feel the growing power of the youthful Jedi protégé Luke. The young and old are in conflict with one another throughout, just as innovative and traditional modes of film-making are set against one another in the creation of the film's distinct aesthetic. On the one hand, *Empire* borrows from the past, for example, by referencing traditional stop-motion techniques, or with Han and Leia's whiplash bickering reminiscent of 'Fred [Astaire] and Ginger [Rogers] fighting up to the last reel', in what Carrie Fisher called 'romance in celluloid'.[107] On the other, it used computerized motion-controlled cameras to create new visual effects and resisted narrative closure. Released in 1980 as the US and UK transitioned into a new decade, as well as an election period in the former and a new government in the latter, the tension between different temporalities in *Empire* creates pervasive uneasiness.

From the opening crawl onwards, the viewer is told that they are entering an ominously 'dark time'. The bright, twin suns of Tatooine in *Star Wars* have given way to the dark enclosures of the corridors on Hoth, the Gothic carbon-freezing chamber of Cloud City, and the shadowy dark of Dagobah. On the swamp planet, the differences between the older and younger characters becomes most visible as Luke seeks out the wise old Jedi master, Yoda, who is 900 years old compared to Luke's nineteen. During their first meeting, Luke is dismissive of Yoda and the creature's capabilities as the young man fails to realize that his new mentor might not look like him. Luke then attempts to wrestle a torch away from the inquisitive Yoda's hands, with the pair literally battling over control of the light in a tug of war between the generations. Hence when Yoda reveals his identity, he disturbs Luke's preconceived ideas about who is considered a hero and why (which bear the hallmarks of racism and ableism given that aliens in Star Wars are configured as racialized 'others' and Yoda has a

Yoda wrestles the light away from Luke in their first encounter on Dagobah

Yoda holds the upper hand in his hut, where Luke's size renders him ridiculous

physical disability).[108] Subsequently, Yoda, the old-school puppet that does not rely on computerized visual effects, holds the upper hand, with his age, wisdom, and knowledge of the past winning out over Luke's youthful naïveté. In Yoda's hut the master circles Luke, whose disproportionately large size in the small space is a laughable hindrance – for example, when he hits his head on the ceiling. Yoda pokes Luke with a stick; he pushes Luke through intense physical training; he guides him through the ways of the Force.

Much of Luke's physical training seems redundant: swinging through vines on Dagobah is no more taxing than swinging from ropes under a moving AT-AT on Hoth. And his initial attempts to use the Force result in failure. Whereas Han and Chewie successfully navigate the *Millennium Falcon* out of the exogorth using their faith and intuition, Luke's lack of faith in the Force results in his ship being swallowed by the swamp. Yoda tells him to 'feel the Force' and speaks of energy and flow between natural objects. His words imply that Luke must let go of his reliance on technology (his X-wing, his droid, his military gadgets) and turn to an older and more harmonious order of things to succeed. But his powers remain frightening to Luke: 'I feel cold!' he exclaims in the blue light as he follows the shadowy form of a Force-vision Vader into an

Luke's X-wing crash-lands in the Dagobah swamp, forcing him to cope without technology; Luke sees his own face staring back at him following his duel with Vader in a Force vision; Yoda lifts Luke's ship from the swamp in a rare moment of stability

underground cavern. There, in a dream-like, slow-motion sequence that breaks down the logic of time, Luke decapitates Vader with his lightsaber. When the Sith Lord's mask dissolves, Luke sees his own face reflected back at him; it transpires that his greatest enemy is not the entrenched power of an older generation but rather that a lack of confidence in his own abilities might lead him to the Dark Side.

Yoda, of course, retrieves Luke's ship from the swamp with ease, with the soaring score providing sonic proof of the elder Jedi's abilities. The X-wing glides majestically through the air. At the mid-point in the film, Luke is finally convinced by the Force's power and Yoda's spectacular act marks the transition from one generation to another. Once again, albeit briefly, *Empire* provides a moment of balance and relative stability. Shortly after, however, Luke's premonition of his friends' calamity on Bespin causes him to reject Yoda and Obi-Wan's warnings and depart from Dagobah. He decides to chart his own path against their advice, rupturing the uneasy balance between the old and young, and the past and future, as he does so.

The Rebel realignment

On Dagobah as in the asteroid field as on Hoth, the predominant heroes of *Empire* are white male characters Luke and Han, who between them destroy AT-ATs, outwit Imperial forces, and (at least attempt to) save their friends. But during the film, both characters experience radical shifts in temporality that transform the identity politics of the Rebel Alliance. After Luke faces Force-vision Vader on Dagobah in slow-motion, and Han is forced into stasis in the carbon-freeze chamber on Bespin, the gender and racial politics of the Alliance privilege, for a brief period, *Empire*'s marginalized characters. The film's representation of its only white female lead, and its sole Black male one – alongside a cast of aliens that are 'othered' by their figurative status as characters of colour – remains inadequate and both sexist and racist in its privileging of white maleness. Nevertheless, in an inversion of fairy-tale tropes, Leia,

Lando, Chewie, and the subservient droids Threepio and Artoo form an alliance on Bespin that sees them, as the most oppressed characters in the film, actively work together to conduct a rescue mission.

The depiction of women and minorities in Star Wars has received much scholarly and critical attention.[109] Carolyn Cocca's assessment of Leia, for example, asserts that the Rebel leader is simultaneously a bold feminist presence that challenges the male-dominated status quo and a white, elite, non-disabled princess.[110] However, Cocca's suggestion that Leia does not experience discrimination warrants closer inspection. Leia's first appearance in the shooting script is through the eyes of men. Whereas the viewer sees Han from their own subjective position ('the rider swings rakishly off his lizard and pulls away his googles: HAN SOLO'), Leia's arrival is mediated by the male gaze ('the two men turn to see PRINCESS LEIA').[111] At Echo Base, she stands amid a circle of male Rebel pilots as she gives them instructions. As one of the men challenges her authority, the viewer sees Leia from outside the group in an over-the-shoulder shot that draws attention to her physical vulnerability in the masculine environment. And then there is her relationship with Han. Throughout the film, Leia repeatedly falls over and requires Han's assistance to right herself, whether in a collapsing corridor on Hoth or tumbling into his arms in the *Falcon*. His insistence on physically overpowering and kissing her despite her protestations ('I am nice men') demonstrates a lack of respect for her autonomy and consent.

In response, Leia frequently attempts to gain an advantage over her male colleagues with barbed yet witty ripostes. Her admonishments of 'scruffy looking nerf-herder!' and 'I'd sooner kiss a wookiee!' are oft-repeated lines of dialogue among fans that raise a laugh and also diminish Han's power over her. However, within the logic of the Star Wars universe, her remarks are bound up in racism and upper-class elitism as she attacks racially 'other' species (Wookiees) and lower-class labourers (herders) with her insults. If she is a feminist icon in a historical sense, she is one of white-centred,

Leia's vulnerability is visible even when she is in a position of authority; Leia falls into Han's arms on the *Millennium Falcon*; Han overpowers Leia before he kisses her

middle-class, second-wave feminism. That is not to suggest that fans cannot or should not love Leia; after all, she is a fictional character, and given the white, patriarchal genesis of the script, it may be that *she's* not bad, she's just written that way.[112] Similarly, Lando's representation is troubled by his misogyny (he objectifies Leia, asking 'what have we here?'), and his overt sexualization of her is in keeping with white stereotypes of Black men threatening racial purity. His attention towards her is unwelcome, yet Han's far more aggressive romantic interactions with her are acceptable to Leia and thus the viewer. Consequently, when she takes Han's proffered arm over Lando's on Bespin, it makes her appear safe rather than endangered.

Lando and Han both offer Leia an arm in Cloud City on Bespin; Lando demonstrating care for Han

The film's racist subtext is further demonstrated by white Luke's defiance of the figuratively black (costume; voice) Vader: 'I will not become a slave to the Dark Side!' Luke shouts. A white, 'Light' and morally good character under threat of slavery from a black-coded Dark and morally evil one inverts the historical truth of racialized power in the US and the UK. Vader, therefore, is terrifying because he evokes a world in which black people hold power over white. Nama does find some redeeming features in the film, though, citing Lando as a successful and 'upwardly mobile black character' who balances his loyalties to the Cloud City people he protects, his alliance with Vader, 'the other "black" character', and his friends.[113] Moreover, Lando repeatedly demonstrates care to those around him. He checks on Han's vital signs in the carbon freezing chamber. He attempts to keep Leia and Chewie safe. And he responds to Chewie with compassion following the bounty hunter's attempt to strangle him. As Billy Dee Williams said about the character, Lando does subvert some white racist stereotypes and insists on challenging 'that old point of view'.[114]

Following Han's immersion in the carbon-freezing chamber and kidnap by Boba Fett, Leia, Lando, Chewie, and the droids (who serve their human masters seemingly without the advantages of citizenship rights) embark on a recovery mission together. Accordingly, the Rebel characters in *Empire* put aside their differences to form a more progressive new alliance. Thus, it is a white woman, a black man, a

Leia, Lando, Chewie, Threepio, and Artoo – the most marginalized characters – embark on a mission to rescue Han

racially othered wookiee, the camp-coded and disabled Threepio, and pet-like Artoo that save the day. The irony of their service to white male characters who need rescuing cannot be overlooked. However, their collectivism resists the trope of the sole authority figure (usually Han) dictating instructions to a subservient crew. Lando saves Leia and Chewie from Vader by aiding their escape. Chewie saves Threepio by caring for and carrying the dismantled droid. Artoo saves all of them by hacking the Cloud City computer and clearing their path to the *Falcon*. Once they are aboard the ship, Lando and Chewie collaborate to fix the hyperdrive, Artoo assists Threepio and Leia, and Chewie and Lando take turns at the

Artoo saves the Rebels at Cloud City by hacking the computer system; Leia, Lando, and Chewbacca at the controls of the *Millennium Falcon*

ship's controls. As Yvonne Tasker argues, space flight in Star Wars 'is understood for the most part as a masculine business' that I suggest tends to be white, too.[115] As such, the Rebels' realignment in the final third of the film works to disrupt the trajectory of the otherwise traditional, patriarchal narrative and gives greater agency to the film's marginalized characters.

I am your (queer) father

In the prison cell on Bespin where Han is tortured by Vader, Leia remonstrates with Lando for giving away their location to the Empire. But, as Lando reassures her, Vader is only interested in Luke and Han: 'Vader doesn't want you at all.' The Black-coded male villain, then, is not interested in the film's sole female protagonist.[116] The Black-coded male villain only wants men. The Black-coded male villain in Star Wars is queer. For while on the one hand the film enables its most oppressed characters to assume power, it cuts off the other hand entirely with its depiction of deviant characters as LGBTQ+ (which I refer to here as 'queer' to embrace a broad spectrum of orientations that are not explicitly articulated within or by the franchise).[117] In fact, the disturbances that upset spatial and temporal stability, that create visual and narrative conflict, and that generate tension between the Dark Side and the Light are all coded as queer.

Drawing on Sara Ahmed's work, I read Empire's entire aesthetic within a framework of queerness. Ahmed writes that, 'to make things queer is certainly to disturb the order of things'. In doing so, queer people turn away from a 'straight' path: 'the queer subject within straight culture hence deviates and is made socially present as a deviant'.[118] With its movement along space diagonals, canted frames, extreme high and low angles, and oblique-shaped sets, as well as deviant characters, Empire, then, is anything but straight. Jack Halberstam also theorizes queerness in spatial and temporal terms. For them, queer time and space (which emerged as a concept within gay communities during the AIDS crisis in the 1980s) is not only about the 'threat of annihilation' but also living 'a life unscripted by the conventions of family, inheritance, and child rearing' in the spaces 'that others have abandoned'.[119] As such, there is a degree to which the Rebels exist within a framework of queer deviance as they dart around the galaxy in a makeshift, but by no means conventional, family unit and find sanctuary in hostile spaces, such as Hoth and Bespin, that are abandoned.

However, it is the Dark Side that is most obviously, if implicitly, coded as queer. For example, the male Emperor is played by a woman, demonstrating a kind of gender fluidity that makes the character dangerous to heteronormative culture. Neither the Emperor nor Vader express any particular interest, sexual or otherwise, in Leia. And, playing to homophobic stereotypes, the two Sith Lords are notably older men who seek to lure the young, handsome Luke to the Dark Side – the queer side – of the Force. Hence, when male members of the Rebel Alliance come into contact with Imperial forces the heroes are endangered by their entrapment in queer temporalities. Luke, for instance, experiences slow motion in the distorted time of a Force-vision on Dagobah in which he confronts, and fears becoming like, Vader. Han, too, is thrust by the Empire into queer time when he enters stasis in the

Luke and Vader clash in a slow-motion sequence of queer time

carbon-freeze chamber. Inert and disrupted, Han becomes another casualty of queer greed as he is sold by Vader to Boba Fett (and indeed to the viewer as a neatly submissive consumable on-screen toy). Even camp Threepio (whose highly feminized demeanour is a homophobic stereotype rendered safe by humans' control over him) succumbs to queer time when he is dismantled by Imperial troops on Bespin. All in bits, he has to be deactivated, which sets him outside of functioning, heteronormative time.

The fight scene between Luke and Vader is the climax of the battle between the not-quite-straight Rebels and the sexually deviant Dark Side. The pair dance around the surreal, hellish underbelly of

Luke chases after Vader in a visually anxiety-inducing shot; the Black- and queer-coded Darth Vader tries to entice Luke to the Dark Side

Bespin, with the intense red and blue light saturation and dramatic diagonal lines of pipework punctuating the steamy scene. Amid the electric hum of their clashing lightsabers, a low-angle frame disorients viewers as Luke chases after Vader. Finally, with Luke clinging to a vertiginous platform suspended high up in a wind tunnel, Vader cuts off the hero's hand, effectively castrating Luke as he is forced to drop his weapon. Carrying the weight of his queerness and Blackness in his dominant stance above the young Jedi, Vader's famous line is a multifaceted plot twist. 'No, *I* am your father': it is an immaculate conception and a motherless birth; he is a Black father, and a queer father, too. Yet as Hannah Hamad argues, paternity is 'the dominant paradigm of movie masculinity'.[120] Thus, it is in claiming paternity that the Sith Lord maintains his terrifying power as a figure of Blackness, queerness, and deviance. And, of course, at the end of the film, the realigned Rebels, who are now devoid of their white male leaders, have still not overcome – or indeed, straightened out – the horror that Vader represents. A new equilibrium is established by their return to proscenium-arch framing as Luke, Leia, and the droids watch Lando and Chewie depart on the *Falcon* from the safety of the Rebels' haven. But Vader is still out there, and his power disrupts the conventional Hollywood happy ending.

A new equilibrium of sorts is restored by a return to proscenium-arch framing

4 Seeing Star Wars

When the doors opened for the first public screenings of *The Empire Strikes Back* at a minute past midnight on 21 May 1980, a period of intense media hype and fan speculation about the sequel came to an end. Many accounts of the film's history end here, too, with acknowledgments of its box-office success and positive reception among audiences. Yet *Empire*'s exhibition strategy and the dedication and creativity of its fans are integral to its history: without them, it would be a lifeless and unseen object.

Thus, in this chapter, I explore the film's exhibition in cinemas and privilege the stories of audience members who saw the movie or engaged with its paratexts in 1980. Using archival marketing materials alongside reports in the daily press, I investigate how the film's technical specifications disrupted theatres by necessitating projection upgrades. Moreover, tracing viewers' responses through fanzines and personal testimonies, I demonstrate how marginalized people, including many women of colour, were foundational to *Empire*'s success in particular, and the burgeoning Star Wars fandom in general. In doing so, the chapter offers new material evidence in support of Megen de Bruin-Molé's argument that 'women have made up a significant and vocal portion of the Star Wars fanbase from the beginning'.[121] Challenging the widespread perception – that persists to this day – that Star Wars fans were predominantly white and male, I draw on the archive to celebrate the fandom's diversity at the point of *Empire*'s release.

Coming to a cinema near(ish) you
The first footage from *Empire* appeared in the film's trailer alongside the rerelease of *Star Wars* in August 1979. Subsequently, audience

interest was regularly piqued by promotional materials including a 1979 Christmas teaser and another, longer trailer in the Easter period of 1980.[122] According to the distributor's market research, which used trailers and print advertisements to gauge people's interest in the movie, excitement about *Empire* was consistently high among viewers who had seen *Star Wars*, regardless of their age or gender. Notably, the researchers canvassed opinion from equal numbers of men and women in every study, demonstrating women's importance in studio decisions about marketing. Testing one of the trailers, the survey found that 100 per cent of women who were familiar with Episode IV said that they would see *Empire*, with 96 per cent of men making the same claim.[123] There was a degree of optimism, then, among Hollywood executives about the film's chances of financial and critical success. Following months of research and teasers, the marketing campaign began in earnest two weeks before the film's release in 126 70mm-equipped theatres in the US and Canada (with releases in another 700 cinemas on 35mm in June).[124]

According to *The New York Times*, the film's initially 'limited distribution' during the first month was 'designed to generate public interest by the struggle to see the movie', in what they called a '"hardticket" play'.[125] In what may seem like a counterintuitive move, Ashley Boone at Twentieth Century-Fox arranged *Empire*'s distribution strategy to make access to the film harder, rather than easier, for viewers. Meanwhile, through its various subsidiaries and partnerships, Lucasfilm flooded the market with merchandise – and flooded the press with talent interviews and behind-the-scenes features. The print and broadcast advertising campaigns were all-encompassing.[126] In *Rolling Stone*, Timothy White described how the 'multimillion-dollar ad campaign and [...] aggressive merchandising' for the film 'resembles a rock & roll world tour', with the cast 'hustled from Los Angeles to New York to Washington to London to Japan and then on to Australia'.[127] For anyone in the US who listened to the radio, watched TV or read a newspaper, it would have been hard to miss news of *The Empire Strikes Back*'s impending release.

To secure rights to the film as part of the first wave of 126
theatrical screenings, cinemas across the US submitted closed bids
to Twentieth Century-Fox; in the nineteen states where the bidding
model was illegal 'Lucasfilm employees, handcuffed to prints of
the film, were dispatched as couriers' in early May 1980.[128] The
terms for exhibitors securing *Empire* were steep: a 90 per cent
return on the movie's box office after the theatre had met its basic
operating expenses, distributor-controlled minimum payments,
and a guaranteed run of sixteen to twenty weeks.[129] Moreover, any
theatres securing a first-wave release date had to provide facilities
for 70mm projection and new Dolby sound systems. Writing in
The Washington Post, journalist Gary Arnold recognized that 'this
picture must have inspired a considerable amount of conversion to
the enhanced presentation around the country'.[130] Indeed, theatres
winning successful bids not only faced the expense of paying the
distributor but also the costs associated with upgrading equipment.
Paul Kershner, a cinema manager in Washington, DC, described how
before receiving the *Empire* print his premises had undergone 'a face
lift', with 'new carpet, patched plaster and state-of-the art sound and
projection equipment'.[131] While the cost of screening *Empire* was
probably prohibitive for many theatres, for those that could afford
the conversion the financial returns on the sequel to the highest
grossing film of all time were likely to be high.

Empire is for *everyone*

Empire opened to great fanfare at its Royal premiere on 20 May
at the Odeon Leicester Square in London, with Princess Margaret
among the celebrity guests.[132] Following its general release on 21
May, it grossed $9,034,000 in just six days (setting an industry
record for per-theatre takings in a multi-city opening) and it out-
performed the opening of *Star Wars* by 66 per cent.[133] By 18 August
it had taken a 'sensational' $11,000,000 in international box office,
too, with $3,497,000 accrued in seven weeks at the Odeon Leicester
Square and just three weeks in other 'provincial' English theatres,

as well as successful runs in South Africa and Japan.[134] The film received cultural accolades, as well. Director Irvin Kershner and producer Gary Kurtz were invited to the Italian premiere of the film at the Venice Film Festival on 19 September.[135] And, in a display of soft power in keeping with the production's military antecedents, President Carter screened the movie for Chinese Vice President Geng Biao, who was visiting the White House to secure trade agreements.[136] From royal attendees to art-house galas, *Empire* had prestige status that belied its blockbuster, family-friendly origins.

Among Star Wars fans, excitement to see the film grew and by 7.00 pm on 20 May 'about 300 people had lined up' outside the Egyptian Theater in LA.[137] To pass the time, 'some played Monopoly, others juggled oranges, ate pizza pies, and still some others played the theme from *Star Wars* on their kazoos'. Fan Terri Hardin, who recalls the queue at the Egyptian, recounts how playing Dungeons and Dragons was a popular pastime, with fans crossdressing in Star Wars costumes, sharing food from coolers and sleeping under Star Wars blankets.[138] Queues sprang up outside many first-run theatres across the US and prompted writer Marcy Moran Heidish to write a guide to good line-waiting etiquette: 'Meet a friend, bring a book, take an amusement you don't mind pursuing in public. People have been observed playing Hearts and Go Fish [...] and there's a rumor about a Ouija board.'[139] Her observations also point to the class and other markers of diversity among audiences, as she writes that 'reading runs from Plato and Hegel to Agatha Christie and Stephen King, *Cosmopolitan* to the *New York Review of Books*. Several *Flying* magazines have been sighted. Crossword puzzles abound'. Finally, Heidish gave some important advice. 'DON'T QUIZ THE OUTCOMERS: When the show before you gets out, don't ask the last audience how the movie ended.' Star Wars spoiler warnings, it seems, were essential even in 1980.

A report from the queue outside the K-B Theatre in Washington, DC, provides insight into the film's broad appeal. According to an article in *The Washington Post*, Petty Officer First Class Mike

Goalen travelled for hours to see the show to ensure that he saw *Empire* before shipping out on military duty. He attended a screening alongside 'computer programmers and economists and housewives and students out of school for the summer', as well as a woman with her four-month-old baby and two other mothers 'who wrote notes to get their kids excused from school'.[140] In LA, queuers to see the film included Josie Figeroa, 'a legal secretary who saw *Star Wars* 68 times and arrived at the *Empire* screening dressed in a homemade copy of Princess Leia's costume'; Judy Johnson, a secretary who came to the show dressed in a Han Solo uniform; and Leslye Wintrob, who was outfitted as a member of the Imperial Forces.[141] At a special benefit screening at the Kennedy Center, Timothy White reported that one of the film's biggest fans was a Yoda-obsessed child called Amy Carter, who 'just loved him and the way his ears wiggled'.[142] Other attendees included graphic designer Deirdre Jepsen, the Rev. Diane Nagorka, who bought eleven tickets for the film, and Terrie LaBarbera, a computer systems analyst who spoke of her impatience to see the film: 'I went to see *Star Wars* the first day too.'[143] What is remarkable to me about the reports is that so many female viewers are present in the queues without journalists ever discussing gender. In 1980, the fact of women Star Wars viewers was so normal as to be wholly *unremarkable.*

Women were not only present in the lines to see the film but also prominent in the franchise's fandom. For example, at the front of the queue at the Egyptian Theater, Terri Hardin waited for three days to secure the first ticket for the movie. Having seen *Star Wars* 181 times (using surreptitious costume changes in the Chinese Theater bathrooms to facilitate her repeat visits), she was understandably eager to see the sequel.[144] An *Associated Press* report noted that she was 'one of those standing in the drizzle outside [...] "The Force is with us and it's going to carry us right on into that theater"', she said.[145] As interest in *Empire* grew, Hardin became something of a celebrity, with local restaurants sending her food and a Lucasfilm staffer helping to keep her spot at the front of the line.[146] According to the *Los Angeles Times*, when the doors opened for the first screening, Hardin 'excused herself from her friends. As she walked to the rear of the auditorium there were cheers: "Terri, Terri, Terri!" Hardin's voice was hoarse. She estimated this was her 25th interview since she first stepped in line.'[147]

In an interview conducted for this book in 2019, Hardin suggests that her presence provoked high-fives rather than chants. Nevertheless, her presence in the Star Wars community was a positive and notable one, and she gave an award-winning cosplay performance with her handmade Yoda puppet at conventions. She recalls that audiences enjoyed *Empire* and let out a 'slow roar' in response to the plot twist. 'People like to feel', she says. And with the Star Wars stories, 'sci-fi, horror and fantasy geeks came out of hyperspace' and were able to 'find their place', regardless of their gender.[148] The only annoyance she expresses is at the memory of how the press depicted fans: she recalls that the media 'tried to exploit me as insane', even though seeing the visual effects and artistry on-screen represented 'a career, a goal'.[149] For Hardin, Star Wars and *Empire* fostered an inclusive family of likeminded people, as well as an inspirational pathway into a professional world of creativity. Through her fandom, she achieved her goal to become a puppeteer who worked with, among others, the Jim Henson Company.

While women were active in the Star Wars fandom, there is some evidence of gendered responses to the film. Audience surveys conducted by Cinema Score Card and 'primarily intended for studio marketing departments' record that of the 536 people surveyed exiting *Empire* screenings, 68 per cent of attendees were male and rated the film an average A+, and 32 per cent were women and gave it an average score of A.[150] The report does not indicate the time of day the results were compiled or the location of the surveys – both factors that might affect women's attendance owing to gendered responsibilities such as childcare. However, it does point to lower interest from female cinemagoers and a slightly less positive response to the quality of *Empire* itself. Market research also revealed some biases, although they were more likely the result of gendered socialization, such as the finding that 'a romantic angle was important to women's interest'.[151] Yet, audiences are complicated objects of study. Star Wars fan and nurse Gayle Gordon found that with four viewings under her belt, the sequel was the better movie of the two. 'It's more sophisticated', she said, without any reference to the romantic subplot at all.[152]

In fanzines from the period there is a similarly messy framing of gender, biases, and socialized interests. Fanzines were fan-created magazines that encompassed a range of styles and both celebrated and contributed to a particular object of fandom (although there were crossover zines, too). Star Wars fans produced a range of publications that could reach thousands of readers via postal and fan-convention sales and caught the attention of Lucasfilm, which requested certain titles for archiving and surveillance designed to curb 'slash' or queer readings of Star Wars media.[153] Titles circulating during *Empire*'s production and release included *Skywalker* (edited by Bev Clark, Maggie Nowakowska, and Barbara Green Deer), *Against the Sith* (Tracy and Nancy Duncan), and *Heroine's Showcase* (Barbara Fuchs), with Black women featuring prominently as editors and artists.[154] Noting a gender bias, one male writer asked in a letter to *Alderaan: The Star Wars Letterzine*, 'can someone please tell me why almost all the S[tar] W[ars] zine eds and writers are women?'[155] Offering one suggestion, scholar Abigail De Kosnik proposes that 'fan time' performed by women is a direct resistance to 'the ways that women's time is typically structured and routinised'.[156] Within the fanzines, though, women did not always conform to feminist or even very kind arguments about Leia's character, or the views of other female fans. Many of them preferred the male characters and critiqued the vaguely feminist presence of the Princess. But what emerges from fanzines is a passionate, knowledgeable, and dedicated fandom led by women in the underground and unofficial pages of their home-made presses.

'A Jedi craves not these things ... '

While on-screen Yoda convinces Luke that Jedi do not need material possessions to succeed, Lucasfilm were less inclined to share that ideology when it came to merchandising the film. For example, *Boxoffice* reported that Kenner Toys spent $8 million promoting Star Wars and original *Empire* play sets, and that companies including Coca-Cola, Burger King, and Xerox had plans to issue consumables ranging from stamps to plastic cups.[157] Other items for sale included 't-shirts, hosiery, towels, sheets, drapes, bedspreads, blankets, slumber bags, watches and talking clocks just to name a few'. Six months after the film's release, Judy Mann wrote that 'Christmas, it was clear, would be nothing without some of the various space stations, planets, snow vehicles and space vehicles [...] in *The Empire Strikes Back*, and specifically, Christmas would be a disaster without a tauntaun and Yoda'.[158] The now famous *Empire* Kenner range included ten new action figures (which notably featured minor characters such as the 'AT-AT driver' and Lobot – but not Lando), as well as more advanced toys such as a *Millennium Falcon* featuring a 'Battle Alert' sound and a Yoda hand puppet.[159]

Noting that demand for the Star Wars toys was high, Mann suggests that in the aftermath of *Star Wars*, shops nevertheless had a surplus of Princess Leia toys because no boys wanted them. Some parents picked them up regardless: 'she was better than nothing'.[160] Whereas a visible and vocal contingent of women made up the franchise's adult fandom in the unofficial pages of fanzines, the officially catered for and commoditized arena of childhood play was heavily masculinized by Lucasfilm marketing. For instance, in the *World of Star Wars* book, a collection of articles aimed at children aged between eight and twelve, all of the contributors were men. Each author wrote as if they were addressing boys and reporting direct from the Star Wars galaxy. The writers interwove production facts and scene descriptions with educational content about science and engineering, which are traditionally masculinized fields.[161] There were other official *Empire* media for children, too, with a Star Wars fan club providing an international community of pen pals and a subscription to the magazine *Bantha Tracks*.[162] Prior to the release of *Return of the Jedi* in 1983, National Public Radio also broadcast an *Empire* adaptation that provided another opportunity for fans to relive the film.[163] With the costs of repeat cinema trips potentially prohibitive for families, and without the availability of *Empire* for VHS home viewing until 1984, the film's male-centric ephemera and paratextual media enabled children to play out their love for the galaxy far, far away in domestic spaces beyond the screen.[164]

From studio market research attentive to both male and female viewers, to the subcultural world of women-led fanzines that gave marginalized voices a platform, evidence suggests that the film targeted and reached a diverse audience. But there was a tension between who was allowed to enjoy the film, and how and where people negotiated their enjoyment in its aftermath. Women, people of colour, queer fans and their intersections thereof may have been visible in queues to see *Empire*, but Lucasfilm and entrenched social hierarchies including whiteness and patriarchy limited their representation in both official and unofficial sites of fandom (for example, Lucasfilm tried to censor any queer content in fanzines).[165] As archival evidence suggests, though, through subcultural practices that defied their critics, marginalized viewers and fans have always been active in the history of Star Wars in general, and of *Empire* in particular.

5 Critics Strike Back

A 'new standard for technological wizardry'.[166] A 'slam-bang *and* poetic space extravaganza about the Getting of Wisdom'.[167] Or a 'morally ambiguous psychodrama that simply cannot be sustained by the still cartoon-like characters and plot'?[168] While audiences voted in favour of the film, which, like *Star Wars*, had extraordinary box-office returns that were bolstered by repeat viewings, professional critics were conflicted. Whereas today critics and audiences alike laud *Empire* as the 'best' Star Wars movie, in 1980 its critical reception was uneven, with reviewers' positive responses to the movie's aesthetics disrupted by their negative reactions to its mass appeal and lack of narrative closure. By examining *Empire*'s reception in the daily press and trade papers, my goal is to draw attention to the politics of class, education, and identity that informed its cultural status. I begin by contextualizing the film's criticism within debates about cinema such as genre, blockbusters, and audiences. Next, the chapter analyses which elements of the movie critics praised or censured, and why. And finally, I consider *who* was writing about the film. I propose that *Empire*'s reviews, written almost exclusively by white men, excluded people with more marginalized identities from discussions about the film and so contributed to the masculinized gatekeeping of Star Wars more broadly.

Class wars

Science fiction and other genre films have not always enjoyed critical attention or success, and today disagreements continue over the merits of blockbuster films and their status as cinema. As Bradley Schauer argues, the avant-garde, auteurist branding of *2001: A*

Space Odyssey (1968) worked to legitimize the science fiction genre alongside '[a] new generation of critics who grew up watching 50s science fiction films, and began to explore their sub-textual meanings, making a case for them as intriguing cultural artefacts'.[169] *Star Wars*, though, had an uneasy relationship with New Hollywood due to its family-friendly pop narrative and focus on merchandise. Its big-budget, blockbuster sequel, then, was always likely to meet with doubt from reviewers who were middle class by profession and guardians of good taste by design. Scholar and critic Robin Wood, for example, wrote a notoriously elitist analysis of Star Wars that discounted the possibility of any deep engagement with the texts. He claims that the 'satisfactions' of *Star Wars* are merely 'repeated until a sequel is required: same formula, with variations. But instead of a leap, only an infant footstep is necessary, and never one that might demand an adjustment on the level of ideology.'[170] His criticism of the original trilogy is rooted in his own classist thinking, which wrongly assumes that films with mass appeal only have value as signifiers of broader political concerns and do not have any intrinsic value within the text.

Wood's discussion of the franchise in 1986 demonstrates much of the cynicism that informed *Empire*'s reviews in 1980. For instance, while *Variety* called the movie a 'worthy sequel' to *Star Wars*, the trade paper also noted that owing to the film's position in a growing franchise, the 'only box office question is how many earthly trucks it will take to carry the cash to the bank'.[171] The article suggests that because the movie's success was assured regardless of the aesthetic value of the film, its position in debates about cinema and cultural value were diminished. And, following Lucas's announcement that *Empire* was to be the second chapter in a nine-part serial, Vincent Canby wrote acidly in *The New York Times* that it was 'the second film in a projected series that may last longer than the civilization that produced it. Confession: when I went to see *The Empire Strikes Back*, I found myself glancing at my watch.'[172] His disdain for the ongoing saga is so acute that it obscures whether it was the *idea* of the franchise or the specifics of the film itself that he found so objectionable. Furthermore, critics also noted the paratextual and commoditized nature of Star Wars' success. Kenneth Turan reflected that 'even now, fleets of trucks are moving untold copies of the novelisation everywhere'; Joy Gould Boyum called the merchandising and marketing strategy a 'media blitz'.[173] In the *Village Voice*, Tom Allan explicitly accused the franchise of cynicism: '*Empire* is tartly and calculatedly, especially in its revving up of Dolby stereo into a weapon of subliminal edginess, a PG hard-action movie.'[174] Although commentators were not necessarily critical of Lucasfilm's economic model, reviews on the whole revealed critical ambivalence towards mass-audience cinema.

In the eyes of the word-herders

Judith Martin, reviewing the film for *Newsweek*, neatly encapsulated her simultaneous enjoyment of *Empire*'s aesthetics and contempt for its blockbuster status in her analogy between the movie and junk food. She argued that:

To call *The Empire Strikes Back* a good junk movie is no insult: There is enough bad junk around. And surely we're getting over the snobbery of pretending that it is undemocratic to recognize any hierarchy of culture, as if both low and high can't be appreciated, often by the same people [...] But the total effect is fast and attractive and occasionally amusing. Like a good hot dog, that's something of an achievement in a field where unpalatable junk is the rule.[175]

At first glance, Martin's analysis appears to elevate the film. However, the comparison relegates *Empire* to the high-end of low-status culture: like junk food, it can only be tolerated and consumed occasionally. Martin also implies that there is something morally repugnant about the notion of overconsumption or, indeed, viewers failing to recognize that Star Wars is distinct from high art. Critics did, in general, value *Empire*'s aesthetics, with the special visual effects (a staple of the science fiction genre) coming in for particular praise thanks to the movie's formal innovation. Reporting that 'Empire is even better than the original', Linda Marsa noted how 'the stupendous special effects, once again, are seamlessly executed'.[176] A review in Boxoffice proclaimed it 'a treat for the eyes and ears', with 'never a moment when the screen isn't filled with action, bizarre creatures or fascinating machinery'.[177] Even Turan, who was otherwise critical of the film and the franchise, suggested that Empire was 'often great fun because the special effects are a little short of astounding'.[178] Consequently, the reviews indicate that generic expectations about the technical creativity of science fiction gave critics license to praise the visual effects without undermining their own status as purveyors of high culture.

Moreover, thanks to Kershner's direction – and possibly owing to his reputation as a film-maker with European stylistic tendencies that appealed to bourgeois tastes – reviews rated Empire's world-building. Writing in Newsweek, David Ansen described how 'in any corner of the frame one can discover a delightfully gratuitous detail – a space lizard climbing up a tree, a puff of rocket exhaust, a barely glimpsed robot – that creates a sense of a totally inhabited fantasy world'.[179] Similarly, Marsa found the direction 'intimate' with 'compulsive attention to detail' that defied the usual parameters of a blockbuster film. Stephen Godfrey, meanwhile, praised its 'subtler relationships'.[180] And Gary Arnold enjoyed its darker themes, claiming that 'Empire turns out to be a stunning successor, a tense and pictorially dazzling science-fiction chase melodrama', which interwove generic conventions to produce something new and unexpected.[181] For some reviewers, then, Empire's lack of narrative resolution and departure from their expectations enabled them to position it within a framework of auteurism that was counter to the tropes of blockbuster cinema.

But the same elements that elicited praise from some critics prompted a backlash from others. For instance, The New York

Times found that the darker themes gave the film 'the air of impending doom – one crisis loaded on top of another – which finally becomes monotonous'.[182] The reviewer compared it unfavourably to children's films such as the 1939 *The Wizard of Oz* and Disney's output, complaining that 'the older entertainments had soul as well as spectacle. Maybe the calculation required to make one of these epics drains the soul out of the finished product.'[183] Another proposed that Lucas 'seems to have forgotten that the chief ingredient of *Star Wars*' success was its spirit of fun'.[184]

However, it was the film's open-ended dénouement that most critics objected to, with Jimmy Summers of *Boxoffice* decrying the lack of a satisfying resolution.[185] Gerald Clarke's otherwise positive review in *Time* declared that *Empire* finished 'on a less satisfying and more ambiguous note' than its predecessor.[186] While it was in many ways 'a better film than *Star Wars*, visually more exciting, more artful and meticulous in detail', Clarke proposed that 'one is left with a nagging sense of incompletion, a feeling of being somewhat short-changed'. Fantasy critic Bill Warren similarly found it 'entirely too downbeat', understanding 'the commercial and dramatic reasons in having a cliff-hanger ending', but nevertheless deciding that 'this is so bleak that it *may* have the reverse effect – people may be reluctant to see *Revenge of the Jedi* in hope of avoiding a sad ending'.[187] And Vincent Canby of *The New York Times* complained that the film 'doesn't even have a complete narrative. It has no beginning or end, being simply another chapter in a serial [...] I'm not as bothered by the film's lack of resolution as I am about my suspicion that I really don't care.'[188] Consequently, owing to its hybrid status as a blockbuster film with art-house sensibilities that defied critical and generic expectations, *Empire* was always destined to be divisive among professional tastemakers. It was simultaneously too big to fail, and too big to win.

Aren't you a little short for a film critic?

Critics' cultural biases about genre and narrative were not the only factors in *Empire*'s critical reception, though, and gender and race both came into play, too. In the post-war period in Britain, Melanie Bell reveals how film criticism was 'one of the most gendered pathways in film culture', with women 'dominating the dissemination and circulation of ideas about individual films and cinema more generally'.[189] Bell argues that women's power in the world of criticism lasted until roughly the mid-1960s, when a resurgence in debates about auteurism and '*mise-en-scène* criticism' fuelled by New Hollywood led to a more masculinized discourse and male-dominated field. She discusses how male critics became 'openly derisive of the previous generation singling out women […] for ridicule'.[190] The male-oriented nature of criticism as a professional environment is evident in responses to *Empire*: of the seventeen US reviews consulted in this chapter, only two (equivalent to 12 per cent) were written by women. That film critics tended to be men did not stop women becoming fans of the Star Wars saga. However, owing to patriarchal notions about masculinity and authority, the maleness of the field likely did prevent women from discussing their responses to the movie in mainstream, public forums. Women edited fanzines among dedicated subcultural groups of perhaps hundreds (or, if they were successful, a couple of thousand) followers; men disseminated their opinions in the pages of newspapers with potentially international circulation. As a result, women's critical subjectivity was devalued and relegated to an amateur space that was less visible to the general public, no doubt contributing to the pervasive but nevertheless unfair cultural assumption that women do not or are not qualified to talk about Star Wars.

Furthermore, it seems likely that the identity of professional critics shaped their responses to questions of representation in *Empire*. In the sample of reviews in this chapter (none of which are written by reviewers that reflect on their identity or subjectivity), most demonstrate clear biases towards white male characters. The white male heroes and actors – Mark Hamill and Harrison Ford as Luke and Han – were twice as likely to receive praise as Billy Dee Williams and his character Lando, and four times as likely to be praised as Carrie Fisher and Leia. Fisher was one and half times more likely to receive a bad review of her performance than a good one, whereas the heroic men (Hamill, Ford, and Williams) were six times more likely to be the recipients of good reviews than bad ones.

The statistics do not, of course, demonstrate a direct correlation between the reviewer's identity and their opinion of the characters or performers. For example, one female critic, Janet Maslin, praised Harrison Ford but denigrated what she saw as the lazy stereotyping of Leia and Lando's characters. She dismissed the 'snappish' Leia 'as if someone were concerned with offering positive role models for children' and complained that Lando's characterization was 'exaggeratedly unctuous, untrustworthy and loaded with jive'.[191] And there were some positive comments about *Empire*'s female and Black performers. Marsa argued that Lando was 'played by just the right amount of roguish charm by Billy Dee Williams'.[192] Charles Champlin praised Carrie Fisher, who 'this time seems to have a newly steely turn of mind, a spirited independence'.[193] In a rare moment of positivity about both characters, Michael Sragow enjoyed Fisher playing 'interstellar royalty in the manner of Rosie the Riveter' and called Williams 'an especially welcome breath of soul' who 'soared through his part like a cosmic, comic Super Fly'.[194] Nevertheless, it was Fisher's romantic 'sparks' with Ford that most impressed the critic, and his response to Lando relied on racist stereotypes. Even in moments of positivity, discussions of the characters and performers were undermined by gendered and racialized language.

Negative reviews about the pair did not hold back. In Bill Warren's eyes, the part of Lando called for 'the charm of Clark Gable, but Williams himself, while a good actor, lacks the magnetism necessary'.[195] Furthermore, he argued that 'Lando Calrissian is

flat and uninteresting', and stated that 'whatever the real reason
for casting a Black actor as Lando, producer Gary Kurtz and Lucas
could have found a more appealing performer'.[196] By questioning
the 'real reason' for casting a talented and renowned actor in the
role of Lando, the critic reveals the racism pervasive not only in
film discourse but also US and UK culture. In Leia and Fisher's case,
it was her position of leadership and appearance that came in for
the fiercest and most widespread criticism. She was, according to
Vincent Canby, 'as sexlessly pretty as the base of a porcelain lamp'.[197]
Another writer, working for a student newspaper, commented
that 'one cannot judge her as an actress until she's allowed to do

Carrie Fisher as Leia and Billy Dee Williams as Lando received positive reviews from
some critics but sexist and racist comments from others

something aside from screech orders, just as one cannot judge her looks until she gets rid of the buns in her hair and the dumpy white leather jogging suit.'[198] So incensed was one writer by Leia's 'obstreperousness' and Lando's general presence in the franchise that the reviewer suggested Lucas had produced 'the first space fantasy heralding the demise of Western civilization'.[199] With such explicit misogyny and racism at the core of the negative review, the prophecy now reads like the highest possible compliment – and an early taste of the online Star Wars commentary that accompanied the prequel and sequel films in later decades.

Conclusion

The imbalances in *Empire*'s reception are indicative of the skewed power dynamics of an often elite class of writers influencing the opinions of a mass readership. Writing about a pop cultural phenomenon that refused to fit the narrative of a blockbuster sequel, critics were conflicted about the film's dark themes and unresolved story, its genesis from New Hollywood and art-house traditions, and its cynical marketing strategy. Consequently, in its critical reception as in its production and exhibition, *Empire* disturbed the status quo, and upset reviewers' notions of taste and generic expectation. Moreover, men dominated discourse about the movie in professional and public arenas, which likely contributed to cultural associations between maleness and authority in discussions about Star Wars. Given that racism and sexism persist today among some Star Wars fans (usually aimed at young women and men of colour in the Disney-era films), the legitimization of harmful stereotypes in *Empire*'s criticism has, I suspect, had a lasting and more powerful effect than any negative commentary on the film's aesthetics.[200] If nothing else, it is a reminder to everyone who writes about film to choose their words with responsibility and care for future generations. Fortunately, though, many fans – and indeed, more recent reviews – have helped to alter the narrative and set *Empire* on an altogether different path of reclamation.

6 Number Five at Number One

A risky sequel that was always guaranteed success. A production narrative that emphasized logistical challenges while erasing the labour of marginalized creative talent. A technologically innovative, forward-looking special effects team that was grappling with the practices of the past. And so, the list of *Empire*'s contradictory genesis goes on, looping through a framework of visual disturbance in the form of oblique angles and canted frames, via the historical presence of viewers that disrupt cultural myths about fan identities, to land, skidding to a sideways halt, among conflicted critical discussions of the film.

The Empire Strikes Back is a movie rendered in volatility. It was produced across borders in the last months of centrist and left-wing governments as both the US and the UK made material, if already politically perceptible, shifts to the right. It publicized its military associations with war-like precision at a moment of heightened political anxiety about the outcomes of the Cold War. In doing so, it was a demonstration of ideological and national soft power that simultaneously gave the film-makers cultural capital in a critical environment unfriendly to blockbuster genre films. Yet, in spite of Lucasfilm's reliance on capitalist mechanisms of commodification and the film's conservatism regarding gender and race representation, *Empire* nevertheless recognized the dangers of climate change and ended with a white woman, a Black man, and group of alienated Rebel 'others' coming together to save the day. Every time you think you see the film in its entirety and fix its meaning, the light shifts and casts a shadow and *Empire* appears different again: it is a plot with infinite twists that is revered by both fans and more casual Star Wars viewers.

Nice to see a familiar face

There is no single explanation for *Empire*'s now assured status as a film 'classic', as the people's preferred Star Wars film. In her work on changing audience tastes and home viewing conditions, Barbara Klinger argues that a film's theatrical release is potentially minimized, historically, by its 'extensive "afterlife"', which is created by television broadcasts, video releases, and on other formats such as DVDs that circulate in domestic space.[201] Klinger also notes that as film reissues require updated and retrospective critical thinking, the discourse surrounding a movie will necessarily change over time. Hence, she observes that whereas *Vertigo* (1958) was advertised as a 'classic' on its 1980s rerelease, it was hailed as a far weightier 'masterpiece' for its 1996 restoration.[202] In *Empire*'s case, its multiple reissues and critical afterlife are intersecting factors in its extraordinary popularity.

By the time *Empire* left movie theatres and transferred to the home-viewing market, the film had been through two theatrical rereleases, with an extended rerelease in the summer of 1981 that had around 1,200 prints in circulation.[203] Following its second theatrical run and in the midst of negotiations about its television broadcast, *Empire* sat behind *Jaws* and *Star Wars* as the third highest grossing film in history.[204] It was released by CBS on video formats in 1984, and despite Lucasfilm arguing for a lower price-per-unit, it retailed for $79.98 in a market designed for rentals rather than individual sales.[205] A print advertisement reminded audiences that 'this is one of the biggest films of all time. Don't wait until your dealer is sold out.' They were told emphatically: 'Strike now.'[206] The next notable moment in *Empire*'s exhibition history was a concurrent DVD release and theatrical rerelease as part of George Lucas's digital restoration of the three original trilogy movies in 1997. With the archived prints of the three films in a bad state of repair – the colours had deteriorated, and the celluloid was damaged – a Lucasfilm team spent three years restoring *Empire* frame by frame.[207] Moreover, Lucas decided that prior to the release of the digitally animated prequel

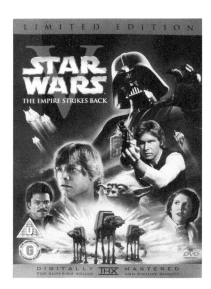

The cover of the rerelease of *The Empire Strikes Back* on special edition DVD, 2004

trilogy, he would have the original films 'fixed' to produce an aesthetic that was impossible with the technology available in the late 1970s and early 1980s. Consequently, Lucasfilm rereleased a digitally enhanced original trilogy with remastered scores, some new shots, and other visual changes.

What followed was a backlash against Lucas and the updated digital versions of the films. In their research into fan-creator relationships, Michael Fuchs and Michael Philips suggest that fans perceived Lucas as guilty of tampering with artworks that were under public ownership.[208] Both *A New Hope* and *Return of the Jedi* faced especial antipathy from fans owing to the substantial narrative and creative differences inscribed through the digital intervention. In the former, film-makers altered the now infamous 'Han shot first' sequence to make bounty hunter Greedo (Paul Blake and Maria De Aragon) the antagonist in the Cantina scene rather than Han. In the latter, an extended musical sequence appeared in Jabba the Hutt's palace. However, while Lucasfilm added 158 new shots to *Empire*, none of the additional material noticeably transformed the film's pace or aesthetic. Most of the changes were limited to inserting shots during the fast-paced battle sequences and erasing the black outlines of the snowspeeders against the white ice on Hoth that occurred in the original compositing process.[209] Critic Roger Ebert noted that 'not much has been changed in this restored and spruced-up re-release'.[210] Consequently, in its digital form, *Empire* was the most *authentic* of the original trilogy films. I argue that as a result, the remastered movie's aura – that is, its visible relationship to the original artwork – emphasizes the qualities of reproduction in the more substantially transformed Episodes IV and VI.[211] *Empire*'s comparative authenticity has contributed to its popularity ever since.

Of course, there are other factors at play. Audiences responded well to the film in 1980, and by 1997 – seventeen years later – a new generation of film critics who had perhaps enjoyed *Empire* as children had begun to replace those reviewers who were ambivalent upon its release. As Fredric Jameson suggests, Star Wars 'satisfies a deep […] longing' to experience the films over and over again.[212] He writes that 'children and adolescents can take the adventures straight, while the adult public is able to gratify a deeper and more properly nostalgic desire to return to that older period and to live its strange old aesthetic artefacts through once again'. The popularity of the original trilogy, therefore, relies on adult nostalgia for childhood simplicity and the simultaneous urge to complicate the films. Moreover, its cultural significance is widespread and extends far beyond online polls and magazine surveys. For instance, Emma Pett's examination of the immersive theatrical experience Secret Cinema observes that its staging of *The Empire Strikes Back* in 2015 enabled the company to access 'subcultural branding', which aligned Secret Cinema with consumers' expert knowledge of the Star Wars franchise and the popularity of Episode V.[213] In doing so, the nostalgia generated by the event crossed generations and spoke to a new wave of fans with different cultural sensibilities who were nevertheless eager to participate in a historic fandom.

Yet it is the attentiveness to authenticity that prevails in critics' responses to the digitally enhanced films and offers the most tangible explanation for *Empire*'s cultural status. For example, *Variety* assured potential viewers that obvious changes to the film were minimal, suggesting that 'this Irvin Kershner-directed sequel is pretty much the same film audiences flocked to 17 years ago'.[214] In the *Hollywood Reporter*, *Empire* was 'unquestionably the best instalment' of the trilogy and 'arguably the crowning achievement of the fantasy-adventure genre'.[215] The revelation that Vader is Luke's father – a plot twist that left many critics in 1980 colder than a frozen tauntaun – had by 2002 become 'a counter thrust that lifted the film into movie history'.[216] Thus, through a kaleidoscope of shifting cultural tastes for authenticity, nostalgia, and critics' childhood familiarity with the source material, *Empire* has become the viewers' canonical, favourite Star Wars film.

Change, it is our destiny

The impact of *The Empire Strikes Back* on US and UK culture is undeniable. It continues to inform film programming, online discourse on social media platforms, and debates about the quality of more recent franchise films. Now, as younger generations of critics and scholars emerge that grew up with the prequel and sequel films as their Star Wars origin stories, I look forward to observing changes in taste and the canonical reification of the movies in future. I anticipate that the prequel films, so often dismissed by older fans and critics owing to the movies' lack of photographic realism, will generate nostalgia among younger viewers who recall the familiar – and authentic – aesthetic of the digital at the turn of the twenty-first century with fondness. Perhaps it will be the CGI second episode of the prequels, *Attack of the Clones* (2002), or the contentious but critically acclaimed second episode of the sequels, *The Last Jedi* (2017), that will top the polls in twenty years' time.

I for one hope that young people's love for their childhood trilogies does shape the cultural landscape in future. It doesn't matter that their ideas reject the wisdom of the Star Wars elders; they should depart from Dagobah with a spirit of adventure and optimism that is respected by the older generation. As Henry Jenkins argues, fans are 'rogue readers' that 'reclaim works that others regard as "worthless" trash, finding them a source of popular capital. Like rebellious children, fans refuse to read by the rules imposed upon them by the schoolmasters.'[217] Eventually, young fans grow up to be critics, teachers, academics, film programmers, archivists, librarians, and cultural tastemakers. They get to change the rules. Of course, I also hope that we are still talking about *Empire* in twenty years' time and debating the myriad aesthetics, ideologies, and material histories that inform the franchise. Paraphrasing Irvin Kershner in a phrase echoed by Rose Tico (Kelly Marie Tran) in *The Last Jedi*, it's possible to debate because you love, not just because you hate.[218] My final hope for this book, then, is that in critiquing *The Empire Strikes Back* – from its (anti-)queer aesthetic to its astonishing effects and everything in between – I have demonstrated the potential in all of us to love complicated and emotionally charged films while simultaneously recognizing their flaws. For even as *Empire* deviates from my personal politics, I remain invested in its characters and narrative. And even as new generations change the language and direction of Star Wars debate, I have no doubt that *The Empire Strikes Back* is a force that will remain with us all for a very long time.

Notes

1 *The Empire Strikes Back* tops many polls
and lists as people's favourite Star Wars
movie. For example, it is first in IMDb's
poll with over double the number of
votes as its nearest competitor – see 'Poll:
Favourite Star Wars Film', IMDb. Available
online: <https://www.imdb.com/poll/
uLB4Ikfqs20/results?answer=2&ref_=po_
rv>. It tops David Edelstein's ranking of
all the films up to May 2018 – see 'Every
Star Wars Movie, Ranked', *Vulture* 21
May 2018. Available online: <https://
www.vulture.com/2018/05/every-star-
wars-movie-ranked-from-worst-to-best.
html>. Similarly, it is number one in the
Guardian's ranking – see Peter Bradshaw,
'Every Star Wars Film – Ranked!' 24 May
2018. Available online: <https://www.
theguardian.com/film/2018/may/24/
every-star-wars-film-ranked-solo-
skywalker>.
2 Musicians including Madonna and Will
Smith have referenced *The Empire Strikes
Back* (for example, Madonna's video for
Die Another Day (2002), Dir. Traktor, USA
and UK: Moving Picture Company), and
television shows including *Buffy the
Vampire Slayer* ('Conversations with Dead
People', UPN, 2002) and *30 Rock* ('Don
Geiss, America, and Hope', NBC, 2010)
have also referred to the film.
3 See, for example, Peter Krämer, *The
New Hollywood: From Bonnie and Clyde
to Star Wars* (London: Wallflower,
2005); Iain Robert Smith, *Hollywood
Meme: Transnational Adaptations in
World Cinema* (Edinburgh: Edinburgh
University Press, 2017); Sean Guynes
and Dan Hassler-Forest (eds), *Star
Wars and the History of Transmedia
Storytelling* (Amsterdam: Amsterdam

University Press, 2017); and Yvonne
Tasker, 'Women, SF Spectacle and the
Mise-en-scène of Space Adventure in
the Star Wars Franchise', *Science Fiction
Film and Television* vol. 12, no. 1, 2019,
pp. 9–28. Matt Hills suggests that film
theory seeks to distance itself from
the industrial and commercial aspects
of filmmaking despite academia
being 'enmeshed in commercialised
systems of meaning'. See '*Star Wars* in
Fandom, Film Theory and the Museum:
The Cultural Status of the Cult
Blockbuster', in Julian Stringer (ed.),
Movie Blockbusters (London: Routledge,
2003), p. 186.
4 Gregory E. Rutledge, 'Jedi Knights and
Epic Performance: Is the Force a Form
of Western-African Mimicry?', in Peter
W. Lee (ed.), *A Galaxy Here and Now:
Historical and Cultural Readings of Star
Wars* (Jefferson, NC: McFarland, 2016),
pp. 106–37.
5 I am indebted to Donna Haraway's
concept of situated knowledges, which
proposes that feminist objectivity is
embodied, critical, and always aware
of its subjective position. See 'Situated
Knowledges: The Science Question in
Feminism and the Privilege of Partial
Perspective Author(s)', *Feminist Studies*
vol. 14, no. 3, 1988, pp. 575–99.
6 Kimberlé Crenshaw, 'Mapping the
Margins: Intersectionality, Identity
Politics, and Violence against Women of
Color', *Stanford Law Review* vol. 43, no. 6,
1991, pp. 1241–99.
7 Many accounts of the franchise are
officially sanctioned Lucasfilm narratives
that prioritize white men as contributors
to, and consumers of, Star Wars. Even

an academic book chapter by former Twentieth Century-Fox marketing specialist Olen J. Earnest appears to be pre-approved by Lucasfilm in advance of publication (he writes to 'express his appreciation to Sidney Ganis, Senior Vice President, Lucasfilm Ltd., and Thomas Casteneda for their assistance in the preparation of this article'). See 'Star Wars: A Case Study of Motion Picture Marketing', in Bruce A. Austin (ed.), Current Research in Film: Audiences, Economics, and Law, vol. 1 (Norwood, NJ: Ablex Publishing, 1985).

8 bell hooks, Black Looks: Race and Representation (Boston, MA: South End Press, 1992), p. 6.

9 In much criticism and scholarship on Star Wars, creator George Lucas is uncritically designated as an auteur and attributed with all decision-making power over the original trilogy. For example, critic Tim Allen says that 'Lucas, like [Walt] Disney and [David O.] Selznick, is a true auteur from conception to final cut' ('What Empire?', Village Voice 26 May 1980, p. 50). Kevin J. Wetmore is right in his assertion that 'the making of the films is mythic and mythologized by those who write about it', but it is Lucas in particular who is mythologized, despite evidence that contradicts his mythic status appearing within the very scholarship that elevates him. See The Empire Triumphant: Race, Religion and Rebellion in the Star Wars Films (Jefferson, NC: McFarland, 2005), p. 9. In one minor example, J. W. Rinzler, who asserts Lucas's total mastery of the film, recounts how Empire producer Gary Kurtz authorized the expansion of the Millennium Falcon cockpit to accommodate the actors, so that it seems to grow in size between Episodes IV and V. Lucas was not pleased about it

yet was powerless to intervene. See Star Wars The Blueprints: Inside the Production Archives (Bellevue, WA: Epic Ink, 2011), p. 122. Tara Lomax discusses this phenomenon in more depth. See '"Thank the Maker!" George Lucas, Lucasfilm, and the Legends of Transtextual Authorship across the Star Wars Franchise', in Star Wars and the History of Transmedia Storytelling, pp. 35–48.

10 I am paraphrasing Laura Dern's character Vice-Admiral Holdo in The Last Jedi, who is encouraging the Resistance (the sequels' Rebel Alliance) to fight against the tyranny of the First Order (equivalent to the original trilogy's Empire): 'We are the spark that will light the fire that will burn the First Order down.'

11 'Jedi is Not a Religion, Charity Commission Rules', BBC News 19 December 2016. Available online: <https://www.bbc.co.uk/news/uk-38368526>. The Charity Commission ruled that 'Jediism' was not a religion.

12 George Lucas sold Lucasfilm, which owns the rights to the Star Wars franchise, to Disney in 2012. See 'Disney Buys Star Wars Maker Lucasfilm from George Lucas', BBC News 31 October 2012. Available online: <http://www.bbc.co.uk/news/business-20146942>. Industrial Light and Magic is a division of Lucasfilm that is responsible for the films' visual effects and digital animation.

13 See Flash Gordon (1936), Dir. Frederick Stephani, USA: Universal Pictures. The serial has thirteen episodes.

14 For more on generic fluidity, see Sandy Rankin and R. C. Neighbors, 'Horizons of Possibility: What We Point to When We Say Science Fiction for Children', in R. C. Neighbors and Sandy Rankin (eds), The Galaxy Is Rated G: Essays on Children's

Science Fiction Film and Television (Jefferson, NC: McFarland, 2011), p. 2. Susan Sontag discusses the links between westerns and science fiction. See Susan Sontag, 'The Imagination of Disaster', *Commentary*, 1965, p. 42, as well as Geoff King and Tanya Krzywinska, *Science Fiction Cinema: From Outerspace to Cyberspace* (London: Wallflower, 2000), pp. 11–43.

15 Carol A. Crotta, 'Stalking the Star Wars Myth', *LA Herald Examiner* 5 June 1980, p. 1.

16 Christine Cornea, *Science Fiction Cinema: Between Fantasy and Reality* (Edinburgh: Edinburgh University Press, 2007), p. 113.

17 Tara Lomax, '"Thank the Maker!" George Lucas, Lucasfilm, and the Legends of Transtextual Authorship across the Star Wars Franchise', in Sean Guynes and Dan Hassler-Forest (eds), *Star Wars and the History of Transmedia Storytelling* (Amsterdam: Amsterdam University Press, 2017), p. 40.

18 Clyde Taylor, 'The Master Text and the Jedi Doctrine', *Screen* vol. 29, no. 4, 1988, p. 99.

19 *THX1138* (1971), Dir. George Lucas, USA: American Zoetrope.

20 Peter Krämer, *The New Hollywood: From Bonnie and Clyde to Star Wars* (London: Wallflower, 2005), pp. 90–1.

21 Robert A. McLean, 'Toy Maker Strikes Back with Yoda', *Los Angeles Times* 22 June 1980.

22 Howard Maxford, *George Lucas Companion* (London: B. T. Batsford, 1999), p. 78.

23 J. W. Rinzler, *The Making of The Empire Strikes Back: The Definitive Story* (New York: Del Rey Ballantine Books, 2010), p. 10.

24 Greg Kidlay, 'Selling – The Force Has Nothing to Do with It', *LA Herald Examiner* 21 May 1980, p. 4.

25 'Paris Parley Plots Release of *Empire, Star Wars* Sequel', *Variety* 27 February 1980.

26 Saul Cooper, '*The Empire Strikes Back* Breaks House Records in the UK', Twentieth Century-Fox Press Release 24 June 1980.

27 Devan Coggan and Tyler Aquilina, 'Here's How Every Star Wars Movie Did at the Box Office', *Entertainment Weekly* 7 November 2019. Available online: <https://ew.com/movies/star-wars-movies-box-office-comparison/>.

28 *The Eyes of Laura Mars* (1978), Dir. Irvin Kershner, USA: Columbia Pictures.

29 Gerald Clarke, '*The Empire Strikes Back*', *Time* 19 May 1980, p. 67.

30 See, for example, *The Red Shoes* (1978), Dir. Michael Powell and Emeric Pressburger, UK: The Archers; and *All That Heaven Allows* (1955), Dir. Douglas Sirk, USA: Universal.

31 Gary Arnold, 'Darth Vader's Surprise Attack!', *Washington Post* 18 May 1980, p. M1. While some critics enjoyed the horror tropes, other reviewers dismissed them, demonstrating what scholar Vivian Sobchack refers to as the 'uneasy connection' between horror and science fiction which has 'bothered many critics'. See *Screening Space: The American Science Fiction Film* (New York: Lexington Books, 1988), p. 25.

32 Taylor, 'The Master Text and the Jedi Doctrine', pp. 101–2. Furthermore, Carlo Silvio suggests that the original trilogy Star Wars films express and attempt to resolve the 'historical transition' to global capitalism, as human culture was subsumed by the logic of capital and the expansion of centralized financial and communication networks, which are represented onscreen by the Empire. See 'The Star Wars Trilogies and Global

Capitalism', in Carlo Silvio and Tony M. Vinci (eds), *Culture, Identity, and Technologies in the Star Wars Films: Essays on the Two Trilogies* (Jefferson, NC: McFarland, 2007), pp. 55–6.

33 David S. Meyer, 'Star Wars, *Star Wars*, and American Political Culture', *Journal of Popular Culture* vol. 6, no. 2, 1992, p. 103.

34 Stuart Hall, 'The Great Moving Right Show', *Marxism Today* January 1979, p. 14. Thatcher's election on 4 May 1979 (somewhat ironically for a government more readily associated with the power of the Empire) led to the first widely recorded use of a now famous date in Star Wars fans' calendars. Taking out an advertisement in the *London Evening News*, the Conservative Party celebrated with a Star Wars reference – 'May the Fourth Be With You, Maggie. Congratulations'. As recounted by Alan Arnold, *Once Upon a Galaxy: A Journal of the Making of The Empire Strikes Back* (London: Sphere Books, 1980), p. 76.

35 Robin Wood, *Hollywood from Vietnam to Reagan* (New York: Columbia University Press, 1986), p. 162.

36 Ibid., p. 167.

37 Ed Guerrero, *Reframing Blackness: The African American Image in Film* (Philadelphia, PA: Temple University Press, 1993).

38 Taylor, 'The Master Text and the Jedi Doctrine', p. 99.

39 Quentin Falks, 'Another Strike for Gold', *Screen International* 24 May 1980, p. 7.

40 Kevin J. Wetmore, *The Empire Triumphant: Race, Religion and Rebellion in the Star Wars Films* (Jefferson, NC: McFarland, 2005), p. 2.

41 Vivian Sobchack, 'Child/Alien/Father: Patriarchal Crisis and Generic Exchange', in Constance Penley, Elisabeth Lyon, Lynn Spigel, and Janet Bergstrom (eds), *Close Encounters: Film, Feminism, and Science Fiction* (London: University of Minnesota Press, 1991), p. 14.

42 Hans Von Storch and Nico Stehr, 'Anthropogenic Climate Change: A Reason for Concern since the 18th Century and Earlier', *Physical Geography* vol. 88, no. 2, 2006, pp. 107–10. The authors offer an overview of cultural conceptions and responses to climate change from the eighteenth century to the late twentieth century.

43 Adilifu Nama, *Black Space: Imagining Race in American Science Fiction Film* (Austin: University of Texas Press, 2008), p. 14.

44 Ibid., p. 32.

45 Judy Klemesrud, 'A Marriage That Was Made for the Heavens', *New York Times* 3 June 1980, p. 12. Discussing identity in narratives about space exploration, Lorrie Palmer and Lisa Purse contend that 'the story of spaceflight omits women and people of colour in favour of a raced, gendered pseudo-utopia in which white men brave the wilderness to establish a pathway that others may (eventually) follow'. See 'When the Astronaut is a Woman: Beyond the Frontier in Film and Television', *Science Fiction Film and Television* vol. 12, no. 1, 2019, p. 1.

46 In *A New Hope* women's screen time accounts for approximately 15 per cent of the film and incorporates both Leia and Aunt Beru; in *Empire* it increases to 22 per cent despite Leia being the only female character in the movie. See Rebecca Harrison, 'Star Wars Women: The Stats', *Writing on Reels* [Blog], 29 May 2018. Available online: <http://www.writingonreels.uk/blog/previous/2>. On Leia's qualitative representation, see Carolyn Cocca, *Superwomen: Gender, Power and Representation* (London: Bloomsbury, 2016), p. 89.

47 J. W. Rinzler, *The Making of The Empire Strikes Back: The Definitive Story* (New York: Del Rey Ballantine Books, 2010).
48 This was the case on the troubled *Solo* production in 2017–18. See Chris Lee, 'Solo: A Star Wars Story Actor Shares New Details About the Troubled Production', *Vulture* 26 March 2018. Available online: <https://www.vulture.com/2018/03/solo-a-star-wars-story-actor-details-production-troubles.html>.
49 *The Empire Strikes Back Press Book*, 1980, p. 7, Margaret Herrick Library.
50 Ibid., p. 7.
51 Peter MacDonald and Mike Brewster, interview with author, March 8, 2020.
52 John May, *The Empire Strikes Back Collector's Edition* (London: Clanose Publishers, 1980), p. 47.
53 *The Empire Strikes Back Press Book*, p. 6.
54 Chris Brown, 'The Empire Strikes Back Wars: Johnson Fires Imagination', *Screen International* 24 May 1980, p. 12.
55 May, *The Empire Strikes Back Collector's Edition*, p. 60.
56 Joe Nazzaro, 'From Dagobah to Delta City', *Starburst*, Special No. 21, October 1994, p. 57.
57 Madelyn Most, interview with author, 8 March 2020.
58 Ibid.
59 Brown, 'The Empire Strikes Back Wars'.
60 John Brosnan, 'The Star Wars Interviews Part Five: Brian Johnson', *Starburst* vol. 3, no. 2, 1980, p. 39; Bruce Nicholson, 'Composite Optical Photography for Star Wars: The Empire Strikes Back', *American Cinematographer* vol. 61, no. 6, 1980, p. 562.
61 Nicholson, 'Composite Optical Photography', p. 612.
62 Pat Jankiewicz, 'Life After Luke', *Starburst*, Special No. 21, October 1994, p. 11.

63 Julie Turnock, 'The True Stars of Star Wars? Experimental Filmmakers in the 1970s and 1980s Special Effects Industry', *Film History* vol. 26, no. 4, 2014, pp. 121 and 124.
64 Ibid., p. 133. Turnock notes that many of the more experimental film-makers working on the Star Wars films have been left out of official ILM histories.
65 One of the VistaVision cameras was reportedly an old, converted Technicolor camera used to film *Gone with the Wind* in 1939 – Alan Arnold, *Once Upon a Galaxy: A Journal of the Making of The Empire Strikes Back* (London: Sphere Books, 1980), p. 47; see also Rinzler, *The Making of The Empire Strikes Back*, p. 91; Richard Edlund, 'Special Visual Effects for Star Wars: The Empire Strikes Back', *American Cinematographer* vol. 61, no. 6, 1980, pp. 553 and 605.
66 Harrison Ellenshaw, 'Creating the Matte Paintings for Star Wars: The Empire Strikes Back', *American Cinematographer* vol. 61, no. 6, 1980, p. 610.
67 Friedrich Kittler, *Gramophone, Film, Typewriter* (Stanford, CA: Stanford University Press, 1986), p. 191.
68 Ibid., pp. 96–7.
69 'Through the Galaxy from Ice Planet to Bog Planet', *American Cinematographer* vol. 61, no. 6, 1980, p. 558.
70 May, *The Empire Strikes Back Collector's Edition*, p. 41.
71 Ibid., p. 45; see also Arnold, *Once Upon a Galaxy*, p. 35.
72 Ronald C. Goodman, 'Filming the Aerials for The Empire Strikes Back', *American Cinematographer* 61, no. 6 (1980), p. 626.
73 J. W. Rinzler, *Star Wars The Blueprints: Inside the Production Archives* (Bellevue, WA: Epic Ink, 2011), p. 106.

74 Aljean Harmetz, 'Space Sounds for *Empire* had Terrestrial Genesis', *New York Times* 9 June 1980, p. 12.

75 Lee Grieveson describes the conditions of the military-industrial complex as emerging from the complicity between the state and its technological industries – such as cinema – in the early twentieth century. See *Cinema and the Wealth of Nations: Media, Capital, and the Liberal World System* (Oakland: University of California Press, 2018), p. 74.

76 Quentin Falks, 'Another Strike for Gold', *Screen International* 24 May 1980, p. 7.

77 Chris Brown, 'Toying with a Great Idea', *Screen International* 24 May 1980, p. 12.

78 Ivor Beddoes, *The Empire Strikes Back* Shooting Schedules, Chapter II Productions Ltd. Call Sheet No. 8 (Studio), Tuesday 13 March 1979, British Film Institute, p. 2.

79 Sian Barber, 'Government Aid and Film Legislation: "An Elastoplast to Stop a Haemorrhage"', in Sue Harper and Justin Smith (eds), *British Film Culture in the 1970s: The Boundaries of Pleasure* (Edinburgh: Edinburgh University Press, 2012), pp. 17 and 21. Barber notes that the Association of Independent Producers, formed in 1976, was anti-union – thus the politics of the film industry were not indistinct from the growing anti-union rhetoric of right-wing Conservatives who took power during *Empire*'s production.

80 Arnold, *Once Upon a Galaxy*, p. 40. Also contrasting with the UK team's adherence to union rules, Lucas demonstrated a lack of regard for labour organizations in the US, when Lucasfilm was fined $25,000 by the Director's Guild for failing to credit Kershner in *Empire*'s opening titles as per the Guild's rules. See Michael H. Franklin, 'Star Wars Report', Letter to the Editor, *Los Angeles Times* 16 August 1981.

81 Barber, 'Government Aid and Film Legislation', pp. 10–12.

82 Arnold, *Once Upon a Galaxy*, p. 23.

83 *The Empire Strikes Back Press Book*, p. 5.

84 *The Empire Strikes Back* [premiere programme], May 1980, Margaret Herrick Library.

85 A recent and brief biography of Ashley Boone, the pioneering Lucasfilm marketing and distribution consultant with responsibility for the release of *Empire*, points to the erasure of Black film-makers from film history, too. See Scott Feinberg, 'He was *Star Wars* Secret Weapon, So Why was He Forgotten?', *Hollywood Reporter* 6 February 2020.

86 Rinzler credits Eileen Baker, however her husband (who also worked on the film) and various other creative talent have confirmed that Rinzler has made an error. See Rinzler, *The Making of the Empire Strikes Back*, p. 308.

87 Ibid., p. 15.

88 Ibid., p. 41.

89 Leigh Brackett, *The Empire Strikes Back* [original screenplay] (1978), p. 45.

90 Goodman, 'Filming the Aerials', p. 624.

91 Melanie Bell, 'Learning to Listen: Histories of Women's Sound Work in the British Film Industry', *Screen* vol. 58, no. 4, 2017, p. 440.

92 Ibid., p. 455.

93 *The Empire Strikes Back Press Book*, p. 6.

94 Rinzler, *The Making of The Empire Strikes Back*, pp. 90–1.

95 *The Empire Strikes Back* [premiere programme].

96 Giuliana Bruno, *Atlas of Emotion: Journeys in Art, Architecture and Film* (London: Verso, 2002), p. 16.

97 Toby Neilson, 'Different Death Stars and Devastated Earths:

Contemporary SF Cinema's Imagination of Disaster in the Anthropocene', *Science Fiction Film and Television* vol. 12, no. 2, 2019, p. 246.

98 Twentieth Century-Fox, 'Stamina, Invention, Zen, Vegetables – And Courage', in *The Empire Strikes Back Pressbook*, 1980, p. 9, Margaret Herrick Library Production Files.

99 Alan Arnold, *Once Upon a Galaxy: A Journal of the Making of The Empire Strikes Back* (London: Sphere Books, 1980), p. 19.

100 Ibid., p. 95.

101 Sandy Rankin and R. C. Neighbors, 'Horizons of Possibility: What We Point to When We Say Science Fiction for Children', in R. C. Neighbors and Sandy Rankin (eds), *The Galaxy Is Rated G: Essays on Children's Science Fiction Film and Television* (Jefferson, NC: McFarland, 2011), p. 114.

102 Kevin J. Wetmore, *The Empire Triumphant: Race, Religion and Rebellion in the Star Wars Films* (Jefferson, NC: McFarland, 2005), p. 20.

103 Gregory E. Rutledge, 'Jedi Knights and Epic Performance: Is the Force a Form of Western-African Mimicry?', in Peter W. Lee (ed.), *A Galaxy Here and Now: Historical and Cultural Readings of Star Wars* (Jefferson, NC: McFarland, 2016), p. 119.

104 Wetmore, *The Empire Triumphant*, p. 39.

105 David Seed, *American Science Fiction and the Cold War: Literature and Film* (Edinburgh: Edinburgh University Press, 1999), p. 94.

106 Susan Sontag, 'The Imagination of Disaster', *Commentary*, 1965, p. 47.

107 Twentieth Century-Fox, 'Love in a Cold Climate', in *The Empire Strikes Back Pressbook*, 1980, p. 8, Margaret Herrick Library Production Files.

108 Nama argues that the alien creatures in Star Wars are racialised 'others' in a predominantly white universe. See Nama, *Black Space*, p. 28.

109 See, for example, Taylor, 'The Master Text and the Jedi Doctrine'; Nama, *Black Space*; and Mara Wood, 'Feminist Icons Wanted: Damsels in Distress Need Not Apply', in Peter W. Lee (ed.), *A Galaxy Here and Now: Historical and Cultural Readings of Star Wars* (Jefferson, NC: McFarland, 2016), pp. 62–83.

110 Carolyn Cocca, *Superwomen: Gender, Power and Representation* (London: Bloomsbury, 2016), p. 87.

111 Leigh Brackett and Lawrence Kasdan, *The Empire Strikes Back – Script*, Fourth draft, 24 October 1978, pp. 2 and 5, Marcus Hu Collection, Margaret Herrick Library.

112 Here I am paraphrasing another fictional female character, Jessica Rabbit, whose deviance is self-reflexively acknowledged as being the product of her creators, not the character herself ('I'm not bad, I'm just drawn that way'). See *Who Framed Roger Rabbit* (1988), Dir. Robert Zemeckis, USA: Walt Disney Animation Studios.

113 Nama, *Black Space*, p. 32.

114 Timothy White, 'Star Wars Slaves to the Empire', *Rolling Stone* 24 July 1980, p. 37.

115 Tasker, 'Women, SF Spectacle and the Mise-en-scène of Space Adventure in the Star Wars Franchise', p. 22.

116 Christopher Deis discusses Vader's Blackness in 'May the Force (Not) Be With You: "Race Critical" Readings and the Star Wars Universe', in Carlo Silvio and Tony M. Vinci (eds), *Culture, Identity, and Technologies in the Star Wars Films:*

Essays on the Two Trilogies (Jefferson, NC: McFarland, 2007), p. 93.

117 Veronica A. Wilson discusses the links between the Sith and historically marginalized women. See 'Seduced by the Dark Side of the Force: Gender, Sexuality, and Moral Agency in George Lucas's Star Wars Universe', in *Culture, Identity, and Technologies in the Star Wars Films*, pp. 134–52.

118 Sara Ahmed, 'Orientations: Toward a Queer Phenomenology', *GLQ: A Journal of Lesbian and Gay Studies* vol. 12, no. 4, 2006, pp. 543–74.

119 Jack Halberstam, *In a Queer Time and Place: Transgender Bodies, Subcultural Lives* (New York: New York University Press, 2005), pp. 1–7.

120 Hannah Hamad, *Postfeminism and Paternity in Contemporary US Film: Framing Fatherhood* (London: Routledge, 2013), p. 1.

121 Megen de Bruin-Molé, 'Space Bitches, Witches, and Kick-Ass Princesses: Star Wars and Popular Feminism', in Sean Guynes and Dan Hassler-Forest (eds), *Star Wars and the History of Transmedia Storytelling* (Amsterdam: Amsterdam University Press, 2018), p. 221.

122 Marketing Studies, *The Empire Strikes Back – Trailer Test – London*, Twentieth Century-Fox 7 September 1979, p. 1, Olen J. Earnest Collection, Margaret Herrick Library.

123 Ibid.

124 Greg Kidlay, 'Selling – The Force Has Nothing to Do with It', *LA Herald Examiner* 21 May 1980, p. 4; Jimmy Summers, '*Empire* Fever Gripping Industry', *Boxoffice* vol. 116, no. 19, 1980, pp. 1 and 3. Andrew J. Neff reports that there were 126 theatres signed up for the first-wave of screenings, although

there are some minor variations of that figure (125 or 127) reported elsewhere. See 'Empire Soars to $9 Mil in Six Days; $10 Mil Week Seen', *Variety* 27 May 1980, pp. 1 and 8.

125 'Highlights Hollywood: The Empire Strikes It Rich', *New York Times* 1 June 1980, p. 19.

126 Olen J. Earnest suggested in 1985 that media costs for a film launch were equivalent to approximately two-thirds of the entire production budget, which reveals the enormous budget and scope of the planning required to successfully launch a blockbuster film. See 'Star Wars: A Case Study of Motion Picture Marketing', p. 4.

127 Timothy White, 'Star Wars' Slaves to the Empire', *Rolling Stone* 24 July 1980.

128 Kidlay, 'Selling – The Force Has Nothing to Do With It'.

129 Ibid.

130 Gary Arnold, 'Film Notes', *Washington Post*, Style Supplement, 5 April 1980, p. 4.

131 Ibid.

132 'Stars Shine Bright for "Empire" Day', *Screen International* 24 May 1980.

133 Neff, '*Empire* Soars to $9 Mil in Six Days', pp. 1 and 8.

134 Saul Cooper, '*The Empire Strikes Back* Hits $11,000,000 in International Markets', Twentieth Century-Fox Press Release, 18 August 1980, Margaret Herrick Library.

135 Saul Cooper, '*The Empire Strikes Back* Outgrosses *Star Wars* in Puerto Rico', Twentieth Century-Fox Press Release 27 June 1980, Margaret Herrick Library; Saul Cooper, '*The Empire Strikes Back* to be Presented at Venice Film Festival September 6', Twentieth Century-Fox Press Release 14 August 1980, Margaret Herrick Library.

136 George C. Wilson, 'New Military Relationship with China is Developing', *Washington Post* 29 May 1980, p. 17.

137 Art Harris, 'Up to Their Kazoos in the Empire's Line', *LA Herald Examiner* 21 May 1980.

138 Terri Hardin, interview with author, 18 September 2019.

139 Marcy Moran Heidish, 'Line Wars: Learning to Love the Wait', *Washington Post* 30 May 1980, p. 17.

140 Carla Hall, 'Trekking to Star Wars II', *Washington Post*, Style Supplement, 22 May 1980, p. 12.

141 Charles Schreger, 'The Force is with the Fans', *Los Angeles Times* 22 May 1980, p. 1.

142 White, 'Star Wars' Slaves to the Empire'.

143 Ibid.

144 Hardin, interview with author.

145 Jay Arnold, 'Star Wars Fans Wait 36 Hours to get into Sequel', *Associated Press* 21 May 1980.

146 Hardin, interview with author.

147 Charles Schreger, 'Star Wars Fanatics Strike Back', *Los Angeles Times* 26 May 1980, p. 5.

148 Hardin, interview with author.

149 Ibid.

150 Cinema Score Card, 'The Empire Strikes Back', *Box Office* 23 June 1980.

151 Marketing Studies, *The Empire Strikes Back Ad Comparison Study*, Twentieth Century-Fox 2 April 1980, p. 4, Olen J. Earnest Collection, Margaret Herrick Library.

152 Schreger, 'Star Wars Fanatics Strike Back'.

153 Henry Jenkins, 'Star Trek Rerun, Reread, Rewritten', in Constance Penley, Elisabeth Lyon, Lynn Spigel, and Janet Bergstrom (eds), *Close Encounters: Film, Feminism, and Science Fiction* (London:

University of Minnesota Press, 1991), p. 178.

154 All the titles are searchable in fanzine database Fanlore, 'Welcome to Fanlore'. Available online: <https://fanlore.org>.

155 Excerpt from a male fan letter that originally appeared in Jeff Johnston and Allyson Whitfield (eds), *Alderaan: The Star Wars Letterzine vol. 10* (Toledo, OH: Kzinti Press, 1981). See Fanlore, 'Alderaan/Issues 06–10', last updated 27 August 2018. Available online: <https://fanlore.org/wiki/Alderaan/Issues_06-10>.

156 Abigail De Kosnik, *Rogue Archives: Digital Cultural Memory and Media Fandoms* (Cambridge, MA: MIT Press, 2016), p. 159.

157 Summers, 'Empire Fever Gripping Industry'.

158 Judy Mann, 'The Impossible Chore: Tracking *Empire* Toys', *Washington Post Metro* 28 November 1980, p. 1.

159 Kenner Toys, 'Star Wars: The Empire Strikes Back', toy catalogue, 1980, Margaret Herrick Library.

160 Mann, 'The Impossible Chore: Tracking *Empire* Toys', p. 1.

161 For example, see Dr M. F. Marten, 'Robots – From Artoos to Quasars', in Kristine Johnson (ed.), *The World of Star Wars* (Weston, FL: Paradise Press, 1981), p. 9.

162 Lucasfilm, 'Join the Official Star Wars Fan Club', advertisement, publication unknown, c. 1980, Margaret Herrick Library.

163 Tom Bierbaum, 'NPR Signs Deal for *Empire* Radio Series', *Hollywood Reporter* 20 April 1982, pp. 1 and 19.

164 Faye Zuckerman, 'Star Wars Price to be Cut', *Billboard* 4 September 1984, pp. 3 and 61.

165 Jenkins, 'Star Trek Rerun, Reread, Rewritten', p. 178.

166 David Ansen, 'The Force is Back with Us', Newsweek 19 May 1980, p. 105.

167 Michael Sragow, 'The Empire Goes for Broke', LA Herald Examiner 18 May 1980, p. 1.

168 Robert Asahina, 'On Screen', New Leader vol. 63, no. 10, 1980, pp. 20–1.

169 Bradley Schauer, Escape Velocity: American Science Fiction Film, 1950–1982 (Middletown, CT: Wesleyan University Press, 2016), pp. 95 and 122–3. See 2001: A Space Odyssey (1968), Dir. Stanley Kubrick, UK and USA: Stanley Kubrick Productions.

170 Wood, Hollywood from Vietnam to Reagan, p. 163.

171 'The Empire Strikes Back', Variety 12 May 1980, p. 14.

172 Vincent Canby, 'The Empire Strikes Back Strikes a Bland Note', New York Times 13 June 1980, p. 1.

173 Kenneth Turan, untitled, New West 16 June 1980; Joy Gould Boyum, 'A Dazzling Sequel That Loses Charm of the Original', Wall Street Journal 27 June 1980.

174 Tim Allen, 'What Empire?', Village Voice 26 May 1980.

175 Judith Martin, 'The Second Star Wars: Two Views', Newsweek 23 May 1980, p. 17.

176 Linda Marsa, 'The Empire Strikes Back', Daily Breeze July 1980, p. 64.

177 Jimmy Summers, 'The Empire Strikes Back', Box Office 19 May 1980.

178 Turan, untitled.

179 Ansen, 'The Force is Back with Us', p. 105.

180 Marsa, 'The Empire Strikes Back'; Stephen Godfrey, 'Star Wars Sequel a Hit and a Myth', Toronto Globe and Mail 27 May 1980.

181 Gary Arnold, 'Darth Vader's Surprise Attack!', Washington Post 18 May 1980, p. M1.

182 David Denby, '"Star Wars" Strikes Back', New York Times 26 May 1980, p. 67.

183 Ibid. See The Wizard of Oz (1939), Dir. Victor Fleming, USA: MGM.

184 Asahina, 'On Screen'.

185 Summers, 'The Empire Strikes Back'.

186 Gerald Clarke, 'The Empire Strikes Back', Time 19 May 1980, p. 68.

187 The original title of Return of the Jedi was announced by Lucasfilm as Revenge of the Jedi. Bill Warren, 'Warren's News and Reviews', Fantasy Newsletter, August 1980, p. 12.

188 Canby, 'The Empire Strikes Back Strikes a Bland Note'.

189 Melanie Bell, 'Film Criticism as "Women's Work": The Gendered Economy of Film Criticism in Britain, 1945–65', Historical Journal of Film, Radio and Television vol. 31, no. 2, 2011, p. 196.

190 Ibid., p. 199.

191 Janet Maslin, 'Robots Return in Empire Strikes: Star Wars Sequel', New York Times 21 May 1980.

192 Marsa, 'The Empire Strikes Back'.

193 Charles Champlin, 'In the Star Wars Saga, Empire Strikes Forward', Los Angeles Times 18 May 1980, p. 30.

194 Sragow, 'The Empire Goes for Broke'.

195 Bill Warren, '"Empire Strike" is a Hit', Enterprise 25 May 1980, p. 34.

196 Warren, 'Warren's News and Reviews'.

197 Canby, 'The Empire Strikes Back Strikes a Bland Note'.

198 Martin Canon, 'Lucas' Empire Strikes Back and the Force is With Him', Bruin Review 1 September 1980.

199 Richard Grenier, 'Movies: Celebrating Defeat', Commentary vol. 70, no. 2, 1980, p. 58.

200 Bethany Lacina, 'Who Hates Star Wars for its Newfound Diversity? Here are the Numbers', *Washington Post* 6 September 2018. Available online: <https://www.washingtonpost.com/news/monkey-cage/wp/2018/09/06/who-hates-star-wars-for-its-newfound-diversity-here-are-the-numbers/>.

201 Barbara Klinger, *Beyond the Multiplex: Cinema, New Technologies and the Home* (Berkeley: University of California Press, 2006), p. 8.

202 *Vertigo* (1958), Dir. Alfred Hitchcock, USA: Paramount.

203 '*Empire* Reissue Extended 2 Weeks', *Hollywood Reporter* 25 August 1981; Roger Cels, '*Empire* Reissue Among Films on Fox's 1981 Release Slate', *Hollywood Reporter* 22 August 1980, p. 4.

204 John Dempsey, 'Offer *Empire, Star Wars* to TV', *Variety* 21 October 1981.

205 Faye Zuckerman, '*Star Wars* Price to be Cut', *Billboard* 4 September 1984, pp. 3 and 61.

206 CBS Fox Video, 'Reserve Your Copy Now: *The Empire Strikes Back*', advertisement, *People* 15 October 1984.

207 Howard Maxford, *George Lucas Companion* (London: B. T. Batsford, 1999), p. 142.

208 Michael Fuchs and Michael Phillips, 'Part of Our Cultural History: Fan-Creator Relationships, Restoration and Appropriation', in *A Galaxy Here and Now: Historical and Cultural Readings of Star Wars*, ed. Peter W. Lee (Jefferson, NC: McFarland, 2016), p. 227.

209 Daniel Kimmel, 'Cleaned Up *Empire* Follows *Star Trek*', *Variety* 24 February 1997.

210 Roger Ebert, '*Empire* Goes to the Heart of *Star Wars*', *The Outlook Rave!* 21 February 1997, p. 7.

211 For more on the aura and reproduction, see Walter Benjamin, *The Work of Art in the Age of Mechanical Reproduction* (London: Penguin, [1935] 2008).

212 Fredric Jameson, 'Postmodernism and Consumer Society', in *Postmodern Culture*, ed. Hal Foster (London: Pluto Press, 1985), p. 116.

213 Emma Pett, '"Real Life is Rubbish": The Subcultural Branding and Inhabitable Appeal of Secret Cinema's *The Empire Strikes Back*', in *Disney's Star Wars: Forces of Production, Promotion and Reception*, ed. William Proctor and Richard McCulloch (Iowa City: Iowa University Press, 2019), pp. 166–78.

214 Kimmel, 'Cleaned Up *Empire* Follows *Star Trek*'.

215 David Hunter, 'Film Review: *Empire Strikes Back*', *Hollywood Reporter* 21–3 February 1997, pp. 6 and 20.

216 Ian Nathan, 'Retro: The Making of… *The Empire Strikes Back*', *Empire* 1 June 2002, p. 99.

217 Henry Jenkins, 'Star Trek Rerun, Reread, Rewritten', in Constance Penley, Elisabeth Lyon, Lynn Spigel, and Janet Bergstrom (eds), *Close Encounters: Film, Feminism, and Science Fiction* (London: University of Minnesota Press, 1991), p. 172.

218 Kershner's original line is '"it's possible to fight because you love, not just because you hate"'. Alan Arnold, *Once Upon a Galaxy: A Journal of the Making of The Empire Strikes Back* (London: Sphere Books, 1980), p. 15. Tico's line is: 'That's how we're gonna win. Not by fighting what we hate. But saving what we love.'

Credits

Star Wars
Episode V
The Empire Strikes Back
USA/1980

Directed by
Irvin Kershner
Produced by
Gary Kurtz
Screenplay by
Leigh Brackett
and Lawrence Kasdan
Story by
George Lucas
Director of Photography
Peter Suschitzky

©1980 Lucasfilm Ltd.
(LFL)
Production Companies
a Lucasfilm Ltd.
production
a Twentieth Century-Fox
release

Production Designer
Norman Reynolds
Edited by
Paul Hirsch
Executive Producer
George Lucas
Associate Producers
Robert Watts
James Bloom
Production Supervisor
Bruce Sharman
Assistant Production Manager
Patricia Carr
Production Co-ordinator
Miki Herman

Location Manager
Philip Kohler
Assistant to Producer
Bunny Alsup
Assistant to Executive Producer
Jane Bay
Production Assistants
Barbara Harley
Nick Laws
Charles Wessler
Production Accountant
Ron Phipps
Assistant Accountant
Michael Larkins
Set Cost Controller
Ken Gordon
Location Accountant
Ron Cook
Continuity
Kay Rawlings
Pamela Mann
First Assistant Director
David Tomblin
Second Assistant Directors
Steve Lanning
Roy Button
Assistant to Director
Debbie Shaw
Casting
Irene Lamb
Terry Liebling
Bob Edmiston
Operating Cameramen
Kelvin Pike
David Garfath
Assistant Cameramen
Maurice Arnold
Chris Tanner

Second Assistant Cameramen
Peter Robinson
Madelyn Most
Dolly Grips
Dennis Lewis
Brian Osborn
Matte Photography Consultant
Stanley Sayer
Gaffer
Laurie Shane
Rigging Gaffer
John Clark
Lighting Equipment and Crew from
Lee Electric
Aerial Cameraman
Ron Goodman
Assistant
Margaret Herron
Still Photographer
George Whitear
Assistant Film Editors
Duwayne Dunham
Phil Sanderson
Barbara Ellis
Steve Starkey
Paul Tomlinson
Special Visual Effects
Brian Johnson
Richard Edlund
Design Consultant and Conceptual Artist
Ralph McQuarrie
Art Directors
Leslie Dilley
Harry Lange
Alan Tomkins
Set Decorator
Michael Ford

Construction Manager
Bill Welch
Assistant Art Directors
Michael Lamont
Fred Hole
Sketch Artist
Ivor Beddoes
Draftsmen
Ted Ambrose
Michael Boone
Reg Bream
Steve Cooper
Richard Dawking
Modellers
Fred Evans
Allan Moss
Jan Stevens
Chief Buyer
Edward Rodrigo
**Construction
Storeman**
Dave Middleton
Property Master
Frank Bruton
Property Supervisor
Charles Torbett
**Property Dressing
Supervisor**
Joe Dipple
Head Carpenter
George Gunning
Head Plasterer
Bert Rodwell
Head Rigger
Red Lawrence
Costume Designer
John Mollo
Wardrobe Supervisor
Tiny Nicholls
Wardrobe Mistress
Eileen Sullivan
**Make-up and Special
Creature Design**
Stuart Freeborn

Chief Make-up Artist
Graham Freeborn
Make-up Artists
Kay Freeborn
Nick Maley
Chief Hairdresser
Barbara Ritchie
Yoda Fabrication
Wendy Midener
Optical Co-ordinator
Roberta Friedman
Colour Timer
Ed Lemke
Negative Cutting
Robert Hart
Darrell Hixson
**Additional Optical
Effects**
Van Der Veer Photo
Effects
Modern Film Effects
Ray Mercer & Company
Westheimer Company
Lookout Mountain Films
Music by
John Williams
Music Performed by
The London Symphony
Orchestra
(Original Music
Copyright/©1980
Fox Fanfare Music Inc./
Bantha Music)
Music Recording
Eric Tomlinson
Orchestrations
Herbert W. Spencer
**Supervising Music
Editor**
Kenneth Wannberg
Music Recorded at
Anvil Studios (Denham)
Original Soundtrack on
RSO Records

**Sound Design and
Supervising Sound Editor**
Ben Burtt
Sound Editors
Richard Burrow
Teresa Eckton
Bonnie Koehler
Production Sound
Peter Sutton
Sound Boom Operator
Don Wortham
**Production
Maintenance**
Ron Butcher
Re-recording
Bill Varney
Steve Maslow
Gregg Landaker
Dialogue Editors
Curt Schulkey
Leslie Shatz
Joanne D'Antonio
Assistant Sound Editors
John Benson
Joanna Cappuccilli
Ken Fischer
Craig Jaeger
Nancy Jencks
Laurel Ladevich
Foley Editors
Robert Rutledge
Scott Hecker
Foley Assistants
Edward M. Steidele
John Roesh
Sound Effects Recording
Randy Thom
Re-recording Technicians
Gary Summers
Howie [Hammermann]
Kevin O'Connell
Re-recording at
Samuel Goldwyn Studios
(LA, CA)

Dolby Consultant
Don DiGirolamo
Stunt Co-ordinator
Peter Diamond
Stunt Doubles
Bob Anderson
Colin Skeaping
Unit Publicist
Alan Arnold
Assistant Publicist
Kirsten Wing
Aerial Camera System by
Wesscam Camera
Systems (Europe)
Helicopter supplied by
Dollar Air Services
Limited
Pilot
Mark Wolfe
**Cloud Plates
Photographed with**
Astrovision by
Continental Camera
Systems, Inc.
**Snow Vehicles supplied
by**
Aktiv Fischer
R2 Bodies fabricated by
White Horse Toy
Company
Special Assistance from
Giltspur Engineering and
Compair
**Special Visual Effects
Produced at**
Industrial Light and
Magic (Marin County, CA)
Novelization from
Ballantine Books

Studio Second Unit
Directors
Harley Cokliss
John Barry

Director of Photography
Chris Menges
Assistant Director
Dominic Fulford
Second Assistant Director
Andrew Montgomery

Location Second Unit
Director
Peter MacDonald
Director of Photography
Geoff Glover
Operating Cameraman
Bob Smith
Assistant Cameramen
John Campbell
Mike Brewster
**Second Assistant
Cameramen**
John Keen
Greg Dupre
Dolly Grip
Frank Batt
Production Manager
Svein Johansen
Assistant Directors
Bill Westley
Ola Solum

*Production and Mechanical
Effects Unit*
**Mechanical Effects
Supervisor**
Nick Allder
**Location Unit
Supervisor**
Allan Bryce
Senior Effects Technicians
Neil Swan
Dave Watkins
**Robot Fabrication and
Supervision**
Andrew Kelly
Ron Hone

Effects Technicians
Phil Knowles
Barry Whitrod
Martin Gant
Brian Eke
Guy Hudson
Dennis Lowe
Effects Engineering
Roger Nicholls
Steve Lloyd
Electrical Engineer
John Hatt
Electronics Consultant
Rob Dickinson
Model Construction
John Pakenham
Effects Assistants
Alan Poole
Digby Milner
Robert McLaren
Effects Secretary
Gill Case

*Miniature and Optical
Effects Unit*
**Effects Director of
Photography**
Dennis Muren
Effects Cameramen
Ken Ralston
Jim Veilleux
Camera Operators
Don Dow
Bill Neil
**Assistant
Cameramen**
Selwyn Eddy
Jody Westheimer
Rick Fichter
Clint Palmer
Michael McAlister
Paul Huston
Richard Fish
Chris Anderson

**Optical Photography
Supervisor**
Bruce Nicholson
**Optical Printer
Operators**
David Berry
Kenneth Smith
Donald Clark
Optical Line-up
Warren Franklin
Mark Vargo
Peter Amundson
Loring Doyle
Thomas Rosseter
Tam Pillsbury
James Lim
Optical Co-ordinator
Laurie Vermont
Laboratory Technicians
Tim Geideman
Duncan Myers
Ed Jones
Art Director – Visual Effects
Joe Johnston
Assistant Art Director
Nilo Rodis-Janero
Stop Motion Animation
Jon Berg
Phil Tippett
Stop Motion Technicians
Tom St. Amand
Doug Beswick
**Matte Painting
Supervisor**
Harrison Ellenshaw
Matte Artists
Ralph McQuarrie
Michael Pangrazio
Matte Photography
Neil Krepela
**Additional Matte
Photography**
Michael Lawler

**Matte Photography
Assistants**
Craig Barron
Robert Elswit
Chief Model Maker
Lorne Peterson
Modelshop Foreman
Steve Gawley
Model Makers
Paul Huston
Tom Rudduck
Michael Fulmer
Samuel Zolltheis
Charles Bailey
Ease Owyeung
Scott Marshall
Marc Thorpe
Wesley Seeds
Dave Carson
Rob Gemmel
Pat McClung
**Animation and
Rotoscope Supervisor**
Peter Kuran
Animators
Samuel Comstock
Gary Waller
John Van Vliet
Rick Taylor
Kim Knowlton
Chris Casady
Nina Saxon
Diana Wilson
**Visual Effects Editorial
Supervisor**
Conrad Buff
Effects Editor
Michael Kelly
Assistant Effects Editors
Arthur Repola
Howard Stein
Apprentice Editor
Jon Thaler

**Production
Administrator**
Dick Gallegly
Production Secretary
Patricia Blau
Production Associate
Thomas Brown
Production Accountant
Ray Scalice
Assistant Accountants
Glenn Phillips
Pam Traas
Laura Crockett
Production Assistant
Jenny Oznowicz
Transportation
Robert Martin
Still Photographer
Terry Chostner
Lab Assistant
Roberto McGrath
**Electronics Systems
Designer**
Jerry Jeffress
Systems Programming
Kris Brown
Electronic Engineers
Lhary Meyer
Mike MacKenzie
Gary Leo
**Special Project
Co-ordinator**
Stuart Ziff
**Equipment Engineer
Supervisor**
Gene Whiteman
Design Engineer
Mike Bolles
Machinists
Udo Pampel
Greg Beaumonte
Draftsman
Ed Tennler

Special Projects
Gary Platek
Supervising Stage Technician
T.E. Moehnke
Stage Technicians
William Beck
Bobby Finley
Leo Loverro
Edward Hirsh
Dick Dova
Ed Breed
Miniature Pyrotechnics
Joseph Viskocil
Dave Pier
Thaine Morris
Optical Printer Component Manufacturer
George Randle Co.
Camera and Movement Design
Jim Beaumonte
Special Optics Designer
David Grafton
Special Optics Fabrication
J. L. Wood Optical Systems
Optical Printer Component Engineering
Fries Engineering
High Speed Camera Movements
Mitchell Camera Corp.
Ultra High Speed Camera
Bruce Hill Productions

CAST
Mark Hamill
Luke Skywalker
Harrison Ford
Han Solo
Carrie Fisher
Princess Leia Organa
Billy Dee Williams
Lando Calrissian

Anthony Daniels
C-3PO
David Prowse
Darth Vader
Peter Mayhew
Chewbacca
Kenny Baker
R2-D2
Frank Oz
Yoda
Alec Guinness
Ben (Obi-wan) Kenobi
Jeremy Bulloch
Boba Fett
John Hollis
Lobot, Lando's aide
Jack Purvis
Chief Ugnaught
Des Webb
snow creature
Kathryn Mullen
performing assistant for Yoda
Clive Revill
voice of Emperor

Imperial Forces
Kenneth Colley
Admiral Piett
Julian Glover
General Veers
Michael Sheard
Admiral Ozzel
Michael Culver
Captain Needa
John Dicks
Milton Johns
Mark Jones
Oliver Maguire
Robin Scobey
other officers

Rebel Forces
Bruce Boa
General Rieekan
Christopher Malcolm

Zev (Rogue 2)
Dennis Lawson
Wedge (Rogue 3)
Richard Oldfield
Hobbie (Rogue 4)
John Morton
Dak Ralter (Luke's gunner)
Ian Liston
Janson (Wedge's gunner)
John Ratzenberger
Major Derlin
Jack McKenzie
deck lieutenant
Jerry Harte
head controller
Norman Chancer
Norwich Duff
Ray Hassett
Brigitte Kahn
Burnell Tucker
other officers

uncredited
James Earl Jones
voice of Darth Vader

Filmed in
Panavision
Recorded in
Dolby Stereo
Colour by
Rank Film Laboratories
Prints by
DeLuxe

Production details:
Filmed from 5 March
1979 on location on
the Hardangerjøkulen
Glacier (Finse, Norway)
and from 13 March 1979
at EMI-Elstree Studios
(Borehamwood, UK).
Additional filming on
locations in Oregon
(USA) and San Francisco

(California, USA).
Filming completed on 24
September 1979.

Release details:
US theatrical release by
Twentieth Century-Fox
Film Corporation on
21 May 1980. Running
time: 124 minutes.
Rating: PG (MPAA:
26034). Washington, DC,
premiere on 17 May 1980.
Rereleased on 31 July 1981
and 19 November 1982.
UK theatrical release
by 20th Century Fox

Film Co. Ltd on 21
May 1980. Running
time: 124 minutes 15
seconds/11,182 feet.
BBFC certificate: U
(passed 07/05/1980
without cuts). London
premiere on 20 May 1980.

*Star Wars Trilogy Special
Edition*
US theatrical release by
Twentieth Century-Fox
Film Corporation on 21
February 1997. Running
time: 127 minutes.
Rating: PG.

UK theatrical release
by 20th Century Fox
Film Co. Ltd on 11
April 1997. Running
time: 126 minutes 52
seconds/11,417 feet +13
frames. BBFC certificate:
U (passed 05/03/1997
without cuts).

Credits compiled by
Julian Grainger

Glossary of Terms

Canon Star Wars films and television shows

Original trilogy

Episode IV: A New Hope (1977), Dir. George Lucas, USA: Lucasfilm (original title *Star Wars*).

Episode V: The Empire Strikes Back (1980), Dir. Irvin Kershner, USA: Lucasfilm.

Episode VI: Return of the Jedi (1983), Dir. Richard Marquand, USA: Lucasfilm.

Prequels

Episode I: The Phantom Menace (1999), Dir. George Lucas, USA: Lucasfilm.

Episode II: Attack of the Clones (2002), Dir. George Lucas, USA: Lucasfilm.

Episode III: Revenge of the Sith (2005), Dir. George Lucas, USA: Lucasfilm.

Sequels

Episode VII: The Force Awakens (2015), Dir. J. J. Abrams, USA: Lucasfilm/Disney.

Episode VIII: The Last Jedi (2017), Dir. Rian Johnson, USA: Lucasfilm/Disney.

Episode IX: The Rise of Skywalker (2019), Dir. J. J. Abrams, USA: Lucasfilm/Disney.

Spin-offs

Rogue One: A Star Wars Story (2016), Dir. Gareth Edwards, USA: Lucasfilm/Disney.

Solo: A Star Wars Story (2018), Dir. Ron Howard, USA: Lucasfilm/Disney.

TV shows

Star Wars: The Clone Wars (2003–5; 2008–14, 2020), Cartoon Network.

Star Wars: Rebels (2014–18), Disney XD.

Star Wars: Forces of Destiny (2017–18), YouTube.

Star Wars: Resistance (2018–), Disney Channel.

The Mandalorian (2019–), Disney +.

Notable companies

Lucasfilm

An independent production company established by George Lucas in 1971. It is responsible for producing Star Wars screen media, as well as other blockbuster films. Since 2012, Lucasfilm has been owned by The Walt Disney Company.

Industrial Light and Magic (ILM)

A division of Lucasfilm founded in 1975. It is responsible for the visual effects seen in Star Wars and many other screen media.

Twentieth Century-Fox

The Hollywood film studio responsible for distributing the original trilogy Star Wars films.

In-universe terms

AT-AT (aka Walkers)	A large, heavily armoured attack vehicle that looks like a tank on stilt-like legs. They are used by the Empire in a battle against the Rebels on Hoth.
Empire	Led by the Emperor, the Empire and its Imperial troops seek to colonize and dominate the galaxy. The Empire's political imperatives remain uncertain.
Force	A metaphysical energy that binds the universe together. It has both Light (positive) and Dark (negative) sides that can be manipulated by Force-sensitive beings.
Jedi	An order of Force-sensitive knights that aims to bring balance to the galaxy by championing the Light Side. Luke Skywalker, Yoda, and Obi-Wan Kenobi are Jedi.
Millennium Falcon	The ship owned by Han Solo. It is known for its speed and for breaking down at inopportune moments. The ship serves the Rebel Alliance.
Rebel Alliance	A group of human and alien beings, as well as droids, from across the galaxy who are affiliated in their desire to overcome the Empire and restore peace.
Sith	An opposing order of Force users (such as Darth Vader), whose goal is to serve the Empire and rule the galaxy by the power of the Dark Side.
Stormtroopers	The usually white-armoured clone-like army of the Empire.
X-wing	A small, single-person aircraft usually associated with the Rebel Alliance.

Cast of characters

Artoo Detoo	A small droid who serves Luke and communicates with beeps and whistles.
Boba Fett	A bounty hunter who forms an alliance with Darth Vader to kidnap Han.
Chewbacca	A fearless, shaggy-haired ally of Han Solo who serves the Rebel Alliance.
Darth Vader	The black-clad, Force-sensitive Sith lord who brings fear to the galaxy.
The Emperor	The mysterious, hooded figure who rules the Empire.
Exogorth	A giant worm-like animal that the Rebels mistake for a cave inside an asteroid.
Han Solo	A mercenary drawn to the Rebels for financial gain and his love for Leia.

Lando Calrissian	The bold Baron Administrator of Cloud City, a mining colony on Bespin.
Leia Organa	A senator and princess who is a courageous leader in the Rebel Alliance.
Luke Skywalker	An inexperienced farm boy who becomes a Rebel leader and Jedi knight.
Mynocks	The bat-like animals that inhabit the exogorth's cave-like mouth.
Obi-Wan Kenobi	A Jedi knight, he died at the hand of Vader and appears as a Force ghost.
See Threepio	A human-like, gold-plated protocol droid who serves the Rebels.
Tauntaun	The lizard-like animals that the Rebels use like camels on Hoth.
Wampa	A yeti-like creature that attacks Luke on Hoth.
Yoda	The wise old Jedi master who teaches Luke the ways of the Force on Dagobah.

Bibliography

Screen and broadcast media

(for all canon Star Wars media see the Glossary of terms)

2001: A Space Odyssey (1968), Dir. Stanley Kubrick, UK and USA: Stanley Kubrick Productions.

30 Rock (2010), 'Don Geiss, America, and Hope', NBC.

All That Heaven Allows (1955), Dir. Douglas Sirk, USA: Universal.

Birth of a Nation (1915), Dir. D W Griffith, D. W. Griffith Corp.

Buffy the Vampire Slayer (2002), 'Conversations with Dead People', UPN.

Die Another Day (2002), Dir. Traktor, USA and UK: Moving Picture Company.

The Empire Strikes Back Radio Series (1983), NPR.

Ewoks (1985–6), ABC.

The Eyes of Laura Mars (1978), Dir. Irvin Kershner, USA: Columbia Pictures.

Flash Gordon (1936), Dir. Frederick Stephani, USA: Universal Pictures.

The Red Shoes (1948), Dir. Michael Powell and Emeric Pressburger, UK: The Archers.

SPFX: The Empire Strikes Back (1980), Dir. Robert Guenette, CBS.

THX1138 (1971), Dir. George Lucas, USA: American Zoetrope.

Vertigo (1958), Dir. Alfred Hitchcock, USA: Paramount.

The Wizard of Oz (1939), Dir. Victor Fleming, USA: MGM.

Who Framed Roger Rabbit (1988), Dir. Robert Zemeckis, USA: Walt Disney Animation Studios.

Archives

British Film Institute
British Library
Margaret Herrick Library

Star Wars materials consulted

Alinger, Brandon, *Star Wars Costumes: The Original Trilogy* (China: Titan Books, 2014).

Arnold, Alan, *Once Upon a Galaxy: A Journal of the Making of The Empire Strikes Back* (London: Sphere Books, 1980).

Johnson, Kristine (ed.), *The World of Star Wars* (Weston, FL: Paradise Press, 1981).

Lightman, Herb A. (ed.), 'Behind the Scenes of Star Wars: *The Empire Strikes Back*', *American Cinematographer* vol. 61, no. 6 (1980).

May, John, *The Empire Strikes Back Collector's Edition* (London: Clanose Publishers, 1980).

Rinzler, J. W., *The Making of The Empire Strikes Back: The Definitive Story* (New York: Del Rey Ballantine Books, 2010).

Rinzler, J. W., *Star Wars, The Blueprints: Inside the Production Archives* (Bellevue, WA: Epic Ink, 2011).

Steneman, Shep, *The Empire Strikes Back Storybook* (New York: Scholastic Books, 1980).

Selected works consulted

Ahmed, Sara, 'Orientations: Toward a Queer Phenomenology', *GLQ: A Journal of Lesbian and Gay Studies* vol. 12, no. 4 (2006), pp. 543–74.

Bell, Melanie, 'Learning to Listen: Histories of Women's Sound Work in the British Film Industry', *Screen* vol. 58, no. 4 (2017), pp. 437–57.

Bruno, Giuliana, *Atlas of Emotion: Journeys in Art, Architecture and Film* (London: Verso, 2002).

Cocca, Carolyn, *Superwomen: Gender, Power and Representation* (London: Bloomsbury, 2016).

Collins, Robert G., '*Star Wars*: The Pastiche of Myth and the Yearning for a Past Future', *Journal of Popular Culture* vol. 11, no. 1 (1977), pp. 1–10.

Cornea, Christine, *Science Fiction Cinema: Between Fantasy and Reality* (Edinburgh: Edinburgh University Press, 2007).

Crenshaw, Kimberlé, 'Mapping the Margins: Intersectionality, Identity Politics, and Violence against Women of Color', *Stanford Law Review* vol. 43, no. 6 (1991), pp. 1241–99.

De Kosnik, Abigail, *Rogue Archives: Digital Cultural Memory and Media Fandoms* (Cambridge, MA: MIT Press, 2016).

Earnest, Olen J., '*Star Wars*: A Case Study in Motion Picture Marketing', in Bruce A. Austin (ed.), *Current Research in Film: Audiences, Economics, and Law* vol. 1 (Norwood, NJ: Ablex Publishing, 1985), pp. 1–18.

Grieveson, Lee, *Cinema and the Wealth of Nations: Media, Capital, and the Liberal World System* (Oakland: University of California Press, 2018).

Guerrero, Ed, *Reframing Blackness: The African American Image in Film* (Philadelphia, PA: Temple University Press, 1993).

Guynes, Sean and Dan Hassler-Forest (eds), *Star Wars and the History of Transmedia Storytelling* (Amsterdam: Amsterdam University Press, 2017).

Halberstam, Jack, *In a Queer Time and Place: Transgender Bodies, Subcultural Lives* (New York: New York University Press, 2005).

Hamad, Hannah, *Postfeminism and Paternity in Contemporary US Film: Framing Fatherhood* (London: Routledge, 2013).

Haraway, Donna, 'Situated Knowledges: The Science Question in Feminism and the Privilege of Partial Perspective Author(s)', *Feminist Studies* vol. 14, no. 3 (1988), pp. 575–99.

Hills, Matt, '*Star Wars* in Fandom, Film Theory and the Museum: The Cultural Status of the Cult Blockbuster', in Julian Stringer (ed.), *Movie Blockbusters* (London: Routledge, 2003), pp. 202–14.

hooks, bell, *Black Looks: Race and Representation* (Boston, MA: South End Press, 1992).

Jameson, Fredric. 'Postmodernism and Consumer Society', in Hal Foster (ed.), *Postmodern Culture* (London: Pluto Press, 1985), pp. 111–25.

Kittler, Friedrich A., *Gramophone, Film, Typewriter* (Stanford, CA: Stanford University Press, 1986).

King, Geoff and Tanya Krzywinska, *Science Fiction Cinema: From Outerspace to Cyberspace* (London: Wallflower, 2000).

Klinger, Barbara, *Beyond the Multiplex: Cinema, New Technologies and the Home* (Berkeley: University of California Press, 2006).

Krämer, Peter, *The New Hollywood: From Bonnie and Clyde to Star Wars* (London: Wallflower, 2005).

Lee, Peter W. (ed.), *A Galaxy Here and Now: Historical and Cultural Readings of Star Wars* (Jefferson, NC: McFarland, 2016).

Nama, Adilifu, *Black Space: Imagining Race in American Science Fiction Film* (Austin, TX: University of Texas Press, 2008).

Neilson, Toby, 'Different Death Stars and Devastated Earths: Contemporary SF Cinema's Imagination of Disaster in the Anthropocene', *Science Fiction Film and Television* vol. 12, no. 2 (2019), pp. 241–58.

Palmer, Lorrie and Lisa Purse, 'When the Astronaut is a Woman: Beyond the Frontier in Film and Television', *Science Fiction Film and Television* vol. 12, no. 1 (2019), pp. 1–10.

Penley, Constance, Elizabeth Lyon, Lynn Spigel, and Janet Bergstrom (eds), *Close Encounters: Film, Feminism, and Science Fiction* (London: University of Minnesota Press, 1991).

Pett, Emma, '"Real Life is Rubbish": The Subcultural Branding and Inhabitable Appeal of Secret Cinema's *The Empire Strikes Back*', in William Proctor and Richard McCulloch (eds), *Disney's Star Wars: Forces of Production, Promotion and Reception* (Iowa City: Iowa University Press, 2019), pp. 166–78.

Schauer, Bradley, *Escape Velocity: American Science Fiction Film, 1950–1982* (Middletown, CT: Wesleyan University Press, 2016).

Seed, David, *American Science Fiction and the Cold War: Literature and Film* (Edinburgh: Edinburgh University Press, 1999).

Silvio, Carlo and Tony M. Vinci (eds), *Culture, Identity, and Technologies in the Star Wars Films: Essays on the Two Trilogies* (Jefferson, NC: McFarland, 2007).

Sobchack, Vivian, *Screening Space: The American Science Fiction Film*, 2nd edn (New York: Lexington Books, 1988).

Sontag, Susan, 'The Imagination of Disaster', *Commentary* October 1965, pp. 42–8.

Tasker, Yvonne, 'Women, SF Spectacle and the Mise-en-scène of Space Adventure in the Star Wars Franchise', *Science Fiction Film and Television* vol. 12, no. 1 (2019), pp. 9–28.

Taylor, Clyde, 'The Master Text and the Jedi Doctrine', *Screen* vol. 29, no. 4 (1988), pp. 96–104.

Turnock, Julie, 'The True Stars of Star Wars? Experimental Filmmakers in the 1970s and 1980s Special Effects Industry', *Film History* vol. 26, no. 4 (2014), pp. 120–45.

Wetmore, Kevin J., *The Empire Triumphant: Race, Religion and Rebellion in the Star Wars Films* (Jefferson, NC: McFarland, 2005).

Wood, Robin, *Hollywood from Vietnam to Reagan* (New York: Columbia University Press, 1986).